The Mission

Of The Teacher

THE MISSION OF THE TEACHER

By

Richard
Cardinal
Cushing

UT COGNOSCANT TE

ST. PAUL EDITIONS

Library of Congress Catalog Card Number: 62-22007

Copyright, 1962, by the *Daughters of St. Paul*

Printed by the *Daughters of St. Paul*
50 St. Paul's Ave., Jamaica Plain, *Boston* 30, *Mass.*

FOREWORD

This book is composed of a number of addresses given by me on various occasions over the past two decades to groups of educators, especially to Catholic Teachers' conventions. We have entitled the collection, THE MISSION OF THE TEACHER, *since the emphasis throughout is on the role of the Catholic educator in modern America.*

We are all agreed that the end and essence of Christian education is the formation in our students of the perfect image of Jesus Christ. The educational system of the Catholic Church in this country has been devised and developed on the premise that integral education must be essentially religious.

In these times and in this civilization, with its conflict of values, the Church gives the student a complete theory of life, a consistent system of education, the only philosophy which adequately meets the problems of man and nature— and certainly the only philosophy which gives its students that God Who should be the Joy of their youth, the Strength of their age, the Life of their immortality.

So long as they abide in the Faith, so long as it is the stable principle underlying all their mental and cultural growth, Catholic teachers will be the hope of this country and the world, the instruments through which the Church gives the world her greatest service. Through her teachers,

9

the Church will fulfill her great social mission among men: to be the principle of permanence in a world of change; the wellspring of sanctity in the midst of evil; the beacon of idealism in an age of cynicism; a ground for hope in the face of discouragement and mounting fear.

May all students in our educational institutions see in their teachers the devotion and patience of the teaching Christ; the kindness and sweet strength of the teaching Christ; the holiness, the goodness, the love of the teaching Christ. May they learn from them to let their light so shine before men that they may see their radiant goodness and be led by their example to glorify the Heavenly Father.

+Richard Cardinal Cushing.

ARCHBISHOP OF BOSTON

CONTENTS

Christ–The Perfect Pattern

I have been asking myself recently a question which must have occurred to many of you. It is a question which I have heard asked by others—and I find it disturbing. The fact that it can be asked seems to me to prove that something is missing in that education for life which is provided for our students. It is the question of the responsibility of Catholic graduates to the Church. Perhaps it might be more fundamental to speak of the *gratitude* of the Catholic graduate to the Church—why is it apparently so often non-existent? Are there not real grounds for such a special gratitude? If there are, or rather *since* there are, what can we do to make our students more aware of it? This is not a question requiring the marshalling of new ideas by research; it is rather a question of giving a new slant to familiar notions, of using time-honored truths in order to meet new needs. The question of how we can best awaken in our graduates a sense of special devotion to the Church, a special gratitude and consequent sense of responsibility to the Church, need not be answered by calling for a change in the content of our courses or the organization of our schools; it merely calls for a new emphasis, a change in the orientation of some of the things we would have taught and done in any case. *Non nova, sed nove.*

Strangely enough, Catholic educators have directed our thinking towards almost every other point of reference except the one of responsibility on the part of our students to the Church. If we examine the reports of educational conventions we find that papers have been delivered on countless other possible relationships which Catholic education may have. "Catholic Education and its Relation to the State"; "Education for Patriotism"; "Catholic Education and the Development of Social Responsibility"; "Catholic Education and the Spread of Democracy"—these are familiar themes. Actually, none of the papers delivered in development of these special topics reveal any unusual or different understanding of Catholic education itself, either in its essential content or in its normal methods. They ordinarily only call for new directions, the application to new and particular problems of old values and of universal Catholic tradition.

So in this present problem of awakening a sense of personal gratitude to the Church in our students, and, as a result of this gratitude, a greater sense of responsibility to the Church, we probably would proceed most profitably if we reviewed precisely what the Catholic student owes the Church as such—precisely what is its contribution to his education and wherein, therefore, lies the true grounds for the special responsibility the educated Catholic has to the Church.

In many of our courses we have tried to develop a certain sense of indebtedness to the universal, historic Church. The mistake has been, however, that we *departmentalized* our effort, giving a false emphasis to superficial historical facts rather than building on fundamental philosophical causes for them. We have reminded our students of the mighty accomplishments of the Church as an educator in the Old World. We have told them of the origins of the great Universities, of the Catholic beginnings of the universities and schools of Italy, France, Spain, Germany and England. We have rehearsed the roster of immortal names in the story of education, and we have been proud to point out the Catholicism of the greatest and the earliest of those names.

Then we have been disappointed, and a little scandalized, because our students, having heard all these wonders out of the past, did not seem to react with the sense of pride in our educational system and gratitude to the Church that we had hoped to develop. I do not think the reason for their lack of reaction is hard to discover; we might even defend their indifference, or at least explain it, by paraphrasing Hamlet, and asking: *What is Alcuin to them, or they to Alcuin?* Why, in terms of the living for which they must prepare and which is so natural a preoccupation to them—why should they be particularly moved by the thought of Salamanca or medieval Paris, Oxford or Bologna? One suspects that we have too long identified the case for the excellence of our educational system with the memories of these great monuments to it.

We must recognize that right here on this continent, in this century, a new civilization is at work. The old names, the old places have become of historic interest, and within that framework still do much to teach and to inspire. But they have no great power to inflame the loyalties, to capture the imaginations, to awaken response in our students. They are too far removed from the circumstances of life and preparation for life of our students. They may interest the erudite minds or intrigue romantic interest; but the record of the past, the history of our educational achievements and the great names in its story are not sufficient to "sell" Catholic education and the Church itself to our students. We must prove to our students that they are indebted to Catholic education not for a hallowed heritage from the *past* alone, but rather for a dynamic, satisfactory and complete system of education at work in the *present* and capable of preparing them, far better than could any other system, for the special needs of the *future*.

We must prove to them that they are indebted to the *Church*—not of the thirteenth century nor of the Renaissance alone, but here and now in the present-day world. We must make it clear, not merely in our philosophy classes, but in all branches of learning, that permeating all our formal education, vivifying the otherwise dead letter of all our instruction, there is a philosophy, a psychology of education which is unique and indispensable— which produced great results in ages gone by, which can produce them now, and which must produce them in the future. We must make our students see that although our educational system is not based on mere pragmatic premises, it can stand the pragmatic test—and stand it perfectly.

The intrinsic truth and excellence of the Catholic theory of education, the practical value of the system based on that theory—these should be the considerations by which we merit the enthusiastic support of our students.

The famed treatise on "Catholicism in Education" by DeHovre should be read and re-read by Catholic professors and all who plead for Catholic education. It should be especially studied by those who plan the courses in our schools and colleges and who integrate the work of the several departments. DeHovre argues that every system of education is based on a philosophy of life. All education properly so-called is based on a complete philosophy of life. All true education is based on the true philosophy of life.

Such, he asserts, is the great law in the development of educational theory. DeHovre pointed out that here in America the hierarchy has produced one great philosopher of Catholic education. He was Bishop John Lancaster Spalding. Belief in the existence of a natural bond between education and life was the fundamental principle of Bishop Spalding's pedagogy. It may be stated as follows: Real life is a process of education and real education is a life-process.

For Spalding, life is a process of growth, of "ceaseless growth toward God," and to promote this process is the function of education. We learn in order that we may improve life; we educate in order that we may attain the end of life. When we study the arts and the sciences or any other discipline, our aim is to enrich and widen life.

"Education is man's conscious cooperation with the Infinite Being in promoting the development of life. To educate, then is to work with the Power who makes progress a law of living things."

So, for Bishop Spalding life and education are correlative terms. He gave much time and study to the understanding and correct solution of the problems arising from their close relationship. All his writings center on this topic. He was perhaps one of the first anywhere, certainly the first in America to investigate thoroughly the relationship between life and education, in history, in theory, and in practice. And he worked out a satisfactory statement of this relationship. He says: "In educating, as in walking, we have an end in view. In educating this end is an ideal—the ideal of human perfection; and to develop and make plain this ideal is more important than any of the thousand questions with which our pedagogical theorists are occupied." Hence Bishop Spalding used to contend: "A complete theory of education would be a complete philosophy of human nature. A system of education is, in fact, the expression of a universal philosophy, embracing God, man and nature."

I assert that our Catholic colleges and universities—quite as much as our secondary schools—

have failed in too great a degree to realize the full possibilities of the Catholic heritage with which they could have developed a perfect system of education under all these aspects. They have too often departmentalized their philosophy, have too much conformed to the philosophies of others—and so have failed to produce among our alumni a specific family feeling with its resultant warm, family loyalty to their colleges.

If we have imitated the non-Catholic educational world in both the content and the pedagogy of our instruction and hence have no special differences from them, we cannot complain because our students have no *special* attachment to us and to our institutions.

It is especially tragic if we have succumbed to the non-Catholic attachment to "naturalness" in education. On the basis of a valid naturalness, we could build an educational system more perfect than any other and unique in itself. I have mentioned DeHovre's admiration for Spalding; he also points out how much our English-speaking tradition could learn in the theory of education from Cardinal Newman.

Cardinal Newman expected our schools to be "different" in that they produced a specifically Catholic "manner." This manner would be based on nature, it would include the best of the natural, but it would always be better than the best nature could produce.

Newman's familiar maxim was that "the heart of every Christian ought to represent in miniature the Catholic Church," and he considered it the function of education to help it do so. For him Christianity was "the completion of natural virtue"; it is the only spiritual environment in which man's character can attain to full perfection. The importance of such formation is obvious when we reflect that man's powers of knowing, feeling and willing (or acting), which together constitute the sum total of his specifically human activities, not only differ as to their nature and object, but are often in conflict with one another. This lack of harmony is one of the consequences of original sin. To restore that harmony by incorporating man in Christianity, which is "the completion of natural virtue": this, Newman argued, is the task of Catholic character education.

Now, it will be asked, how is this harmony to be achieved? The first step is to recognize clearly the fact that knowing, feeling and willing are three distinct powers of the soul. While related one to the other they must never be confused. Each enjoys a certain autonomy, so to speak. Thinking is not willing, and feeling is not thinking. Catholic education never loses sight of this distinction. The next step is to guide and direct each of these powers aright.

Beginning with the intellect, which is so often confused as it wanders about in a labyrinth of fragmentary truths, Catholic philosophy points out the way that leads to ultimate Truth in which all partial truths find their explanation. Thus unity and harmony are established in the intellectual life of man. The procedure is the same in the case of the will and of the affective life. Left to itself the will may attain to one or other virtue but seems incapable of orienting itself properly in a world where, as Chesterton says, "The virtues have gone mad because they have been isolated from each other and are wandering alone." Catholic moral training will enable this individual to bring these virtues together into a harmonious whole and to lead a truly virtuous life. So, too, with the emotional life. How Catholic education harmonizes the discordant elements here may be seen from the fact that the genuine Christian finds no difficulty in reconciling the fear of God with the love of God.

The complete formation of man, or complete character education, according to Catholic ideals means that each of these faculties is directed to the attainment of its proper object and that all work together harmoniously for the attainment of his eternal destiny. Such an ideal of character is in no sense artificial; on the contrary, as Newman remarks, the educated Christian gentleman is the soul of simplicity and naturalness.

The most challenging task in the formation of character by any educational system nowadays is the organization of the affective life of the individual. Here, too, the Church gives the Catholic student a tremendous advantage, and our educational system should manifest its marked superiority. The concept of "catholicity" implies on the one hand a clear recognition of the proper character and individuality, so to speak, of each of the various life-values and, on the other, due regard for a fixed hierarchy of values. So far as the individual's education is concerned, this means that he has learned to appreciate to some extent, at least, *all* human values and to maintain a due proportion in his devotion to each of them.

As examples of these values we may mention Religion, science, art, literature, society, the Church, the state, the nation, industry, politics, power, virtue, etc. They are the various institutions and activities that go to make up human life and to make it worthwhile. They may be considered as entities, as "goods"; and each is a desirable "good." Together they form an ensemble, an organic whole. Each of them is endowed with a certain character that distinguishes it from the others; each is governed by definite principles; each has a particular function to perform in the life of man. But at the same time, all are organic parts of the whole and as such they must conform to the principles of unity and order by which the whole is governed.

That there are conflicts in the field of values is only too apparent. The devotees of science often refuse to recognize the claims of religion; the cult of the natural sciences leads to a denial of the importance of philosophy and the sciences of the spirit. There are those who would attribute all human progress to the operation of economic factors; those who would identify virtue with knowledge; those who would educate the citizen rather than the man; those who would deny the existence of the supernatural; those who would subordinate the individual to the group; those who would explain the whole of man's life in terms of biology and physiology; those who would substitute some form of culture for the teachings of the Church; those who would render to Caesar the things that are God's. These examples will serve to show what is meant by a distortion of values.

For Catholicism, in the realm of values, there is an *Unum necessarium* and this is true whether we are speaking of the individual or of the whole human race. God is the Value of all values. All else possesses value to the extent that it leads to God. Hence, the central place given to religion in the hierarchy of values. All other human interests must be subordinate to this. This is the contention of Newman, who says: "All things are good in their place; human learning and science, the works of genius, the wonders of nature, all, as I have said, have their use, when kept in subordination to the faith and worship of God; but it is nothing else but an abuse, if they are suffered to engross the mind, and if religion is made secondary to them."

Our students should be constantly reminded, and our teachers should remind themselves, that Catholicism offers the only theory of life capable of producing a theory of education which meets and solves this modern problem of the critical conflict of values in life, in personal life and in social life.

Catholicism gives the student a perfect pattern for the resolution of conflicts in values. It gives him, first of all, that Christ in Whom all perfections are blended and all conflicts are solved.

The embodiment of the Catholic "manner" should be Christ Jesus, and His personality should dominate all our schools. If it does, then He will be the principle of difference between our schools and all others—and the loyalty our graduates have to Him will carry over into their loyalty to our schools.

He dominates our philosophy of life and of education because in Him are united all the attributes of perfection to be found in mankind. In ordinary human beings one or other of these qualities may indeed be met with but it is seldom that the presence of one estimable characteristic is not offset by the absence of others equally desirable. "In His sacred Person, Christ unites the two natures, divine and human. In Him, heaven and earth are brought together. In Him, the majesty of the King of Kings is associated with the humility of the servant of the servants of God. In Him are combined 'the wisdom of the serpent and the simplicity of the dove.' In Him we find the gentleness of the babe and the courage of the hero. He is 'meek and humble of heart,' but as occasion arises He shows what strength of character implies. His enemies more than once felt the sting of His righteous wrath, yet He was a master in the art of self-control. Christ is at once the Way and the Truth; He is the Teacher of Faith and the Guide of reason. He is kindness and goodness personified. He manifests the deepest sympathy and the sublimest self-denial. His love for His fellow-man knows no bounds; it embraces all and is denied to none. Yet it shows none of the weakness, none of the wavering of human love. His mercy impelled Him to grant pardon to the worst offender, yet His own life was marked by an austerity and a spirit of penance that even the holiest of men have found it difficult to approach."

Catholicism also offers a superior system of education because it reveals to the student man as revealed by biology and also man as revealed by theology. No one can be a psychologist unless he be also a biologist, which is to say that without a knowledge of man's animal nature our psychology must necessarily be incomplete. Catholicism has never lost sight of this principle. The definition of man as a rational animal is in accordance at once with Catholic philosophy and with common sense. Yet Catholicism has never made the mistake of reducing psychology to a branch of biology as is done in many modern systems. On the contrary, Catholicism proclaims another axiom which is just as true and just as important, viz: No one can be a psychologist without a knowledge of the teachings of theology. In other words, without a knowledge of God there can be no complete knowledge of the human soul. These two axioms should go hand in hand. "Without the life of grace, the life of the mind is incomprehensible."

Finally, as DeHovre points out with other instances of the Church's unique power to reconcile conflicting truths and values, Catholicism offers the student a system of education inspired by a balanced theory of nature. Other theories are baffled by the apparent conflict between optimism and pessimism. Some enemies of the Church contend that her doctrine entails a disparagement of human nature, while others assert that she attributes an unwarranted dignity to man. As a matter of fact, Catholicism does both, but not exactly in the way her calumniators maintain. The Church preaches both the Fall and the Redemption, sin and pardon, death and resurrection, heaven and hell. There is indeed something terrifying in a sermon on death as delivered by a penitential preacher in the dim light of the altar candles on the opening night of a mission. But on the morrow, as dawn lights up the sanctuary, the same preacher ascends the pulpit and talks to his congregation of the joys of eternal life. In the teaching of Catholicism Jacob's ladder is always represented as reaching from earth to heaven. Life and death, sin and redemption, are invariably linked together. Optimism and pessimism go hand in hand. In the Office of the Dead, the Church repeats the lamentations of Job, including some of the most despairing groans that have ever issued from the human heart; but in the same service she chants the most glorious song of life the world has ever heard: *I am the Resurrection and the Life.*

Here, too, Catholicism manifests its superiority over other systems. It finds no difficulty in reconciling the "opposite virtues," as Newman has so well shown.

One could continue indefinitely the catalogue of conflicts for which the Catholic system of education is prepared to provide. There is the conflict between the one and many in social thought, between the individual and society; there is the conflict between nature and grace, religion and culture; there is the conflict between tradition and progress; between nationalism and internationalism; between the ideal and the real. To the solution of all these conflicts Catholicism brings an intelligible answer, and it does so here and now, today.

It is for this, then, that the Catholic student should be indebted to the Church. Not because the Church gives him beautiful buildings in which to study, or once did. Not because the Church has produced great names and great civilizations in times gone by. But because today, in these times and in this civilization, the Church gives him a complete theory of life, a consistent system of education, the only philosophy which adequately meets the problems of man and nature—and certainly the only philosophy which gives its students that God Who should be the Joy of their youth, the Strength of their age, the Life of their immortality.

Surely if they are brought to the understanding of this *difference* in the Church that builds their schools and colleges, our students will acquire a deeper and more enthusiastic loyalty for our institutions.

Religion–Indispensable in Education

I must always speak as a priest. [1] In so doing,
however, I feel at home with you, for there is probably no profession more kindred to that of the priest
than the profession of the teacher, and the bonds
of mutual sympathy between the priest and the
professor should, it seems to me, be many and powerful. Perhaps that mutual sympathy should be the
beginning of the collaboration in the kindred work

[1] Given to the Association of American Colleges.

of religion and of education for which I make a plea. Perhaps we cannot expect to accomplish for some time yet much more than the development of that *sympathy* and of a mutual respect one for another, but if we accomplish at least *that*, we shall have made a great step forward over the present sad condition which too often prevails between the respective forces which you and I represent.

I refer, of course, to the condition of estrangement that sometimes exists and seems to be increasing between organized education and organized religion, between the priest (to the extent that he is a symbol of the Church) and the professor (again to the extent that he is the symbol of the school or college). Clergy and professors usually are good friends; usually clergy are themselves scholars, at least incidentally—and not infrequently teachers and professors take their places among the most devout members of the average American community. The estrangement to which I refer is not a question of personalities or of differences between individuals; it is a question of chasms yawning between systems, systems of education and systems of thought, chasms which must somehow be bridged for the good of both religion and education, and, I might add, for the good of that democratic way of life which depends so vitally on the contributions to it that religion and education have to make.

I suppose it is generally conceded that religion alone, or its product in the human person, piety, is not enough to make a complete citizen; devout and saintly souls do not always prove the most alert and effective members of the civil community. It must be equally clear that education alone, at least in the sense of the mere transmission of knowledge, is far from being sufficient to produce the complete citizen of a democracy. Irresponsibility, flagrant disregard for the basic codes of conduct which underlie personal integrity and social order, all these, far from being limited to the uneducated, are, in fact, present in tragic degree even among the educated. It is not at all certain that marital loyalty is greater among the educated than among the simple; it is by no means certain that civic sense is more highly developed among the well-educated than it is among the average members of the normal community; it is the distressing fact that international crimes are more often than not perpetrated by nations in which education is not merely generally available but is even more or less of a fetish. World War II, for example, did not start among primitive or uncouth peoples; in cold, historical fact, it was planned, pushed forward and waged by highly educated peoples, by peoples who bent their scientific and other knowledge to the criminal purposes of the greatest crime in history. Whatever else may be said of them, no one can accuse them of neglecting education. Indeed, they exalted education, mere education and especially education without religion, to a level more lofty than that of almost any modern people.

I have never been able to understand the position of those Americans who deliberately seek to isolate religion from education. We are told that education should be for *life,* that education should be related to living. We are told that to live is to act, that education should therefore be related to action. But human action is necessarily *moral* action, and therefore education for action, for living, for life, should certainly include moral education. But we are told that education should be without moral preoccupations in a secular democracy, that at most our modern state can tolerate only a purely secular ethic; that no moral teaching in our secular schools can include elements or sanctions taught by centuries of religious inspiration which are behind all our social values and our democratic institutions. Religion has not merely been departmentalized in the educational system of our secular society—that would be evil enough. But religion is actually proscribed, ruled out, as being without reference to the personal ends or social objectives of modern education. Yet, if our reasoning be correct, religion, or at the very least religious morality, is indispensable to the very notion of modern education. There is no adequate morality without religious values; without morality there is no truly human action. Human action embraces all living–and education, we are told, should govern living. *Education should be for life.*

But in the same breath we are told that education should be purely secular, that it should be non-religious.

This insistence that education be without religious inspiration and religious elements, even on the part of those who speak of the relationship between education and integral living, constitutes one of the most baffling contradictions of all our modern social, moral and educational thinking. Every now and again one encounters in the newspapers declarations from one or another "liberal" clergyman who opposes, with no little passion and appeal to principle, the introduction of religion into education, the entrance of the Church into the field of education whether with her own schools or with an offer to collaborate with the schools of the State or other agencies.

Now there are many reasons why one might oppose certain forms of religious teaching in secular schools. One might conceivably protest it in the name of religion itself and the desire to keep religion undefiled and undiluted. On such grounds Catholics have sometimes felt obliged to make real reservations with regard to many proposals made for religious and moral instruction in non-religious schools. The conscientious reservations of many non-Catholics are based, I have no doubt, on like religious considerations.

But what *is* unintelligible to the rest of us is the opposition of those clergymen, religious leaders, who take their stand against efforts to solve the critical problem arising from the strictly non-moral character of purely secular education. Such clerical opposition, usually labelled "liberal," is unintelligible not only because of its source, but also because of the premises on which it purports to be based. Almost always when proposals are made for bringing moral teaching into schools, or for collaboration between Church and school on however limited a basis, these "liberal" clergy and others assert that such proposals militate against "civil liberties" and compromise our American policy of the separation of Church and State.

We are all, I hope, sensitive to the necessity for vigilance over our civil liberties. We must be constant in our civil viglance, constant and uncompromising. But I see no reason to believe that we are more aware of our civil liberties or better appreciative of what civil liberties are than the members of other democratic societies which have settled the issue of religious education in their schools and colleges without essential compromise of the rights of Church or State, and have done so in a spirit of collaboration, to the immense benefit of their democracy.

Similarly, we all, I think, recognize the realistic considerations which render necessary our American policy of the separation of Church and State. It is true that the organized State and the organized Church here in America are completely separated; however, the citizen, the subject of the State, and the moral believing person, the subject of the Church, *cannot be separated.* Citizen and believer are blended in one personality; education fashions and perfects personality. State and Church, the forces which make for citizenship and those which make for morality, simply must find some formula under which to cooperate if education is to do its integrating work, if it is to escape becoming not merely *secular* but positively materialistic. There is no way out of that dilemma. There is none known to history, none known to reason and none known to modern experience.

The extremes to which the concept of the separation of Church and State is pushed by self-styled "liberals" are particularly noticeable, I repeat, in the field of our common interest: education. These extremes are *fantastic* and *un-American.* One hesitates to imagine where they may lead us; school boards may soon be asked to "purge" any and all courses in Dante, Chaucer, Milton, Tennyson, and for that matter, most representative poets. In fact, if the completely secular point of view represents the ideal in these matters, then history and political science courses may have to rewrite the Declaration of Independence, Lincoln's Gettysburg Address, and the basic documents of our political, as well as cultural, tradition. So much of Western thought in the past twenty centuries has been impregnated with the spirit of Christianity and its God, that if it is to be banned on the ground that it is *religious teaching*, it is hard to see what there will be left to teach. The Church might not consider this to be religious teaching at all, certainly not adequate religious teaching. But a secularist might, and his appeals might have far-reaching effects on the needs and the rights of the rest of the community!

The result of all this has been that our American schools and colleges have lost all their religious tone and content in the sense that their tone may once have been Christian. But in another direction they have very definitely acquired a "religion," that they very clearly reflect and even teach. The "religion" of our secular colleges is the *religion of secularism*. For all its negative character, it has just as truly an *attitude* with regard to such religious questions as the existence and nature of God, the norms of morality, the claims of Revelation and the like, as Judaism or Christianity. While it prevents traditional religion from expressing itself in education, secularism has managed to "take over" quite completely the curricula of our elementary, secondary and collegiate levels of education. It has done so largely by invoking the American policy of the separation of Church and State, a policy which it has made the cloak and the screen of its own religious attitude and objectives.

The distinguished American educator, Doctor Nicholas Murray Butler, once observed how the religion of secularism had managed to achieve its present exclusive hold on tax-supported schools; his observation holds for many other educational institutions where religion has been relegated for about the same reasons to some incidental place in the history or sociology courses. Doctor Butler said: ". . . an odd situation has been permitted to arise. The separation of Church and State is fundamental in our American political order, but so far as religious instruction is concerned, this principle has been so far departed from as to put the whole force and influence of the tax-supported school on the side of one element in the population, namely, that which is pagan and believes in no religion whatsoever . . . . The government's indifference to religion must not be allowed to become opposition to religion."

I have called this extreme development of the idea of separation of Church and State "fantastic."

I think it is also profoundly un-American. The concept of education which our founding fathers followed was neither indifferentist nor unreligious. The colony of Massachusetts is an example at hand. In 1654 a law was passed that no one who had shown himself "unsound in the faith" was to be employed in the schools. A little later, every grammar school master had to be approved by the minister of the town and of the two adjacent towns, not presumably, because the children of these towns would attend the school, but to make sure of the master's orthodoxy. Calvinistic training ran through the whole system, both in books and internal administration: morning and evening prayers were required in the schools and usually there were catechism classes conducted by the minister some time during the week. On Mondays pupils were asked for a summary of the Sunday sermon—summaries which doubtless called for acts of humility from those eminent divines. The Calvinistic system of training was continued by the Latin schools and the academies that began to flourish in the post-Revolutionary period. By a little stretch of terminology, it might be said that the public schools in the East were Protestant parochial schools up to the Civil War, and even later. Colleges were all sectarian, most of them schools of divinity, and they realized their aims better than they do today, that is to say, they came nearer to educating the whole

man, nearer to imprinting on society the mark of
the educated leader. The point is that American
educators on every level, and especially on the level
of liberal arts, once recognized the essential con-
nection between religion and morality, between
morality and responsibility and democracy. In 1939
this American tradition found expression in a program published by the American Council on Education. It said: "To be well-governed in a democratic
way . . . (people) must be intellectually enlightened.
But this enlightenment might prove more a bane
than a boon if it is not translated into moral action.
For moral action, there is only one rational basis,
namely, the conviction of our accountability to the
Power that gave us being. The Brotherhood of Man
is an idle dream unless there is a recognition of the
Fatherhood of God." This is American language; it
bespeaks the necessity for religious education on
every level of our instruction. The President of Yale
University spoke with perhaps even greater clarity
and cogency in 1937 when he said: "If our historical
studies have taught us anything it is that selfish
materialism leads straight to the City of Destruction. To fight it we have need of clear intelligence.
We have no less need of unswerving loyalty to the
Golden Rule. . . . I call on all members of the faculty, as members of a thinking body, freely to recognize the tremendous validity and power of the
teaching of Christ in our life-and-death struggle

against the forces of selfish materialism. If we lose in that struggle, judging by present events abroad, scholarship as well as religion will disappear." That, too, is American language; and quite as eloquently as would the words of a bishop or a priest, this speech of the President of Yale bespeaks the strict necessity of religious education on every level of instruction.

Such education is not, however, being provided in our schools and colleges. It is ruled out of tax-supported schools on the premise we have already discussed. The secularization of elementary and secondary education has carried over into the collegiate education provided in State and private colleges alike. Here, too, religion has been not merely departmentalized in our liberal arts and other curricula, it has been consciously eliminated or unconsciously neglected. Herein lies the root cause, to one man's way of thinking, of the two saddest problems of education in America: 1) The social sterility of the courses which our colleges *do* offer, and 2) the increasingly obvious failure of our colleges to produce well-rounded, dynamic leaders of the *responsible* society that a democracy should be.

I do not know what solution of this problem will eventually commend itself to State schools, to private institutions, or to non-Catholic educators. I am certain their best thought is being devoted to finding a solution acceptable to them. But I do know the solution which Catholics have been forced to devise.

We have long decided that to secure for religion its needed place in integral and democratic education we must undertake to provide our own educational system, primary, secondary and collegiate. The effort to do so has been Herculean; it has demanded energies on the part of our leaders and sacrifices on the part of our people which would be utterly out of proportion, indeed indefensible, did we not count the purpose so high. For conscience' sake and in order to save what we know to be necessary for moral education, we have submitted to a system of double-taxation and material disadvantages which one critic did not hesitate to call "the most substantial and dramatic act of faith in education that is being made by any section of the American populace." The educational system of the Catholic Church in this country has been devised and developed on the premise that integral education must be essentially religious, that man is at once a rational and a religious animal, that if either reason or religion be neglected he tends to be more an animal than a man, more a menace to society than a member of it. But, despite its Catholic religious tone, this system, according to a Protestant author, adheres in most respects to the early American model, the educational system inspired by the American conviction with regard to the true relation between religion and life to which we have already referred.

We strive to remember in all our instruction, scientific, liberal arts, or sociological, that God is the Reality of reality itself; that even with the most complete knowledge and love of all things else, God is still the supreme object of human knowledge, human love and human striving; that all men are created in the image and likeness of God, though made imperfect even in their created natures by sin; that men remain free, despite sin, and capable of co-operating with God's grace unto their personal perfection and the regeneration of their society; that to do either we must know and love our fellowmen and all other creatures both in themselves and in their relation to the true cosmos, a cosmos not limited to the material order but to all of earth and heaven, purgatory and hell; that within this cosmos there are spiritual forces both good and evil the knowledge of which is no less important than the knowledge of the laws of matter; that there is a purpose to individual lives and to history itself; that the City of Man is interrelated with the City of God; that God's Providence operates in human events and that He is not far from us since in Him we live and move and have our being; that education should prepare us in the light of all these truths to master the nature which is below us in order to achieve the nature which is above us; that education should give us a knowledge of all things such as to enable us to utilize nature unto our comfort and convenience and liberty, but especially unto the liberty we have as the sons of God, not merely sons because His creatures, but sons because sharers, potentially, at least, of the life and love and the liberty by which God Himself is divine. It is our Catholic conviction that the liberal arts are not truly liberalizing unless they include the influence of these truths, the truths which, as we see it, both liberalize and *liberate* the human spirit from the things which otherwise enslave and degrade men and nations. We are confident that the integration with the liberal arts tradition of these religious truths in no wise limits or deforms the tremendous natural validity of that tradition. On the contrary, we consider that it was out of the blend of these truths, the religious truths provided by revelation, and the rational truths of the liberal arts, that Western Civilization came into being, the civilization which made Christendom and which gave our society the last true unity it had.

Education will not be able to do its most urgent work of helping restore unity to our broken society until education has come to terms with these spiritual values once again. This conviction is not limited to Catholics; indeed, one wishes that Catholics appreciated it as vividly as they should and gave it the militant expression that it is receiving from sensitive non-Catholics all over the world. Writing of the intangible world which religion opens up to the liberal arts student, a professor of economic history at the University of Chicago has written: "What was the secret of the unity, of the comparative harmony during the age when Western Civilization began to expand? Harmony and unity are the great needs of the twentieth century. In so far as our ancestors managed to achieve them, it was not by means of standardized methods of work or entertainment. It was not by means of large economic units.

"The unity possessed by Europeans in the twelfth and thirteenth centuries was founded on a view of reality that has become dim with the passage of the centuries. Like all men and women always, our European ancestors were concerned with the material conditions of their daily existence and with the strains and occasional joys of their relations with their families and neighbors. But they saw man's place in the universe in a different light from their modern descendants because for centuries the Christian faith had accustomed them to give priority to the spiritual, the immaterial side of their nature. . . .

"As long as Christians generally were convinced of the existence of this reality, and as long as Europeans generally were Christians, they had a less destructible basis for unity than can ever be found in the tangible. The uniformity of external things, through standard products, is no substitute for medieval unity, as a basis for world community. If humanity is starved for charity and love, as today, the physical world, where all is relative, cannot provide them. . . .

"The process of cultural disintegration and of increasingly colossal conflict that has characterized the past half century can be halted, if at all, only by man himself, by supreme efforts of men's wills in the service of cultural unification and understanding. Such a halt depends upon a determined stand by men of good will against the social and cultural and even the economic developments which the technical inventions of mankind, including the use of atomic energy, facilitate. The price of a halt would seem to be once again the establishment of faith among mankind that all are one in Christ, that men have it in their power to become free agents for good, less because of the advances in practical science and technology than in spite of them. If and when they act in the belief that machinery and mechanics could provide them with means of liberating themselves from slavery to the stereotyped existence which machinery and mechanics have created, they will have taken a decisive step towards understanding each other and towards making humanity into a single family."

Here is the practical basis of the need for integration of religion with liberal arts and all education.

Never was unity so ardently desired as today it is. Never was it so tragically needed. Never did those who walk in the tradition of the liberal arts, never did educators and priests generally, have so imperative a mandate to promote the things which make for peace, which foster unity. But let us not be deceived. Humanity does not lift itself by its own bootstraps. We cannot *think* ourselves or *study* ourselves or *lecture* ourselves into unity. HUMAN UNITY IS A MORAL CONCEPT. It is attained through a meeting of *minds* and a blending of *wills*, through the rational and willing acceptance of *law*. Underlying that law must be morality; sustaining morality is religion. Somehow, sometime, by some formula you must find the way to integrate with your liberal arts and other educational programs the contribution to moral and social building, as well as personal perfection, which religion and religion alone can make. *Until* you do, you build in vain who strive to build a human city. *When* you do, then, under God, you will build not merely for time, but for eternity. You will educate not merely the sons of men, but the children of God. You will then be what the professor should always be: no mere purveyor of facts to brains that disintegrate and die, but the inspirer of souls that never die—souls to whom you will be, even as the priest, channels of the Spirit of God, co-founders of the Kingdom of Heaven on earth.

Strengthening Awareness

of Personal Dignity

The voice of the times is the voice of God and we discover much of God's Will for us in the needs of our generation. God's call to our teachers—I dare even say: His mandate to them—in this hour of history, is clearly echoed in whatever states accurately and urgently a genuine need of our children.

By such a norm it is easy to discern the emphasis God would have us give in our conferences and classes for an indefinite time to come. The late Cardinal Muench once pointed out one of the unmistakable challenges to education. He spoke of the way in which secularism is creating an educational situation which can result only in "split personalities," with consequent unhealthy disorders both for individuals and for society.

"It is fatal for the education of a child if education is religious at home and unreligious in the school," the Cardinal said. "Our youthful generation must not become schizophrenic, a generation of split minds and split characters."

In other words, it is disastrous spirituality, disastrous pedagogy and disastrous sociology to educate children in accordance with a system which pretends that God is important on Sunday, but so unimportant that He must not be bothered about or so much as mentioned Monday through Friday from 9 to 3; or pretends that the child has a soul, spiritual and immortal, when he is at home or in church, but becomes a soul-less secular character when he goes to school, so that any mention of God's law, the supremacy of conscience and the guides to the good life of the soul is out of the question in the classroom, indeed *illegal*, a violation of the doctrine, recently elevated to an American dogma by the secularists, of the total and unqualified separation of Church and State.

You and I accept the traditional American system of separation of Church and State not as a warcry against any of our fellow-citizens, but as a formula under which we can live at peace with those

who do not share our faith. But we cannot suppose—
and neither can any honest educators—that all education is to be conceived, planned and conducted
as if separation of Church and State were the sole
and over-riding basis of all intellectual and religious
life.

There are other principles in education than this
largely negative political formula; other principles
which free men as well as men of faith have not
been ashamed to acknowledge hitherto in our history. One of these other principles, far more basic
and pertinent in education, is the principle set forth
in the earliest catechism reflections on the purpose
of all existence: "God made us to know Him, to
love Him and to serve Him in *this* world that we
may be happy with Him in the next."

Nothing could be more basic, more pertinent
or more intimately bound up with the purpose and
nature of education than this statement of the very
reason for a child's existence or the existence of any
one, for that matter. To affirm this principle, as all
believing people must do, on Sunday and to deny
it for all practical purposes thereafter in the school
week—even to forbid reference to it on the grounds
that religious references violate a political theory—
surely this is either hypocrisy or great blindness.

Yet it is precisely this which the secularists require of religious people if their educational systems
are to enjoy the favor of the State. It is asking chil-

dren to ride two mental horses at once, to submit to a contradictory understanding of God, the world and themselves, and it can only lead to the "schizoid" state of mind on all basic matters which Cardinal Muench properly said is the fruit of the secularist requirements in education.

Against all this, you are called to bear an integral witness: to teach the presence of God, His wisdom and His love in all that is and in all that is true, whether on the level of nature or that of grace. Yours it is to teach the unities behind things as well as the special truth, goodness and beauty of each particular branch of learning. Yours to bring sanity as well as salvation into the lives of the children of our generation. Catholic education has a magnificent, a unique contribution to make to minds split by secularism's unhealthy divisions.

The norm of the urgent needs of our generation reveals another special contribution Catholic education can make at the moment. Pope Pius XII clearly pointed out that personality is being smothered in our day by the cancer-like growth of the social collectivity. He described the way in which the Socialist State, present in some degree in every secularist society, chokes the life of anything which it considers less than itself, and it assuredly so considers the individual.

Pius XII remarked that this process of absorbing the individual into the collectivity has now gone on so long that many persons have not merely succumbed to it, but appear to welcome it. And so, the Pope spoke of a "mania for being absorbed into a huge human mass," in the midst of which individual personality is killed.

It is difficult in an age of socialism for any men, even the most otherworldly of Christians, to safeguard their personal dignity and to retain awareness in themselves or acknowledgment from others of their individual significance. And yet, unless education awakens this awareness in the young and strengthens it in all, education will have disastrously failed our generation.

I know not by what means the secularist proposes to offset the totalitarianism in his educational theories, but I do know the spiritual and philosophical emphases by which you and I can and must make our students aware that each of them counts with God Himself and therefore must count before men and nations. In every class, at all times, by every device at our command we must drive deep into the consciousness of our children the idea of the dignity of each soul, the inviolability of each conscience, the reality of each individual destiny. We must keep strong the moral concepts of personal responsibility, the philosophical idea of individual vocation, the dogmatic appreciation that the Son of God came to die out of love for each lonely soul.

Perhaps by these emphases we can do our part, an indispensable part, to counteract the "mania for absorption into the collective mass" and to restore the sense of individual personal dignity.

What else does the voice of God, speaking through the needs of the hour, ask you to emphasize in your teaching? Once again the Holy Father summed up in few and telling words a problem of the age which is a challenge to teachers. Speaking of the manner in which every human faculty and external sense is bombarded in our day by contemporary advertising, television, radio, tabloid papers and picture magazines, Pius XII observed that so unrelenting an assault on eye and ear, to say nothing of nerves, leaves the physical man without rest or refreshment and so compels him to live on the level of the external and the superficial as to prevent concentration on his own inner self. So far advanced is this deterioration of inward life that the Holy Father dared to make this appalling declaration: "A type of man is being developed in our day who cannot stand to be alone with himself and his God for even an hour!"

The observation is completely true. Which of us does not perceive it? Who can deny that it is disastrous, ruinous to personal happiness and to social culture? Nothing could be more evil than the spread of that desolation which lays waste the world when no man thinketh in his heart.

It is clear that education has a work to do here which can be done nowhere else. With all the other arts we teach, we must include the art of prayer; to the crafts we must add the techniques of meditation; the science of the saints must supplement all the other sciences our children master. See what a golden opportunity lies open to Catholic educators who are responsive to the needs of the hour, the voice of God!

Do not make the mistake of supposing that you will have many allies in the work of Christian education. Such, alas, is not the case; there is no reason to believe that it will be in the near future. Indeed, the great scandal is that many who present themselves as Christians, aye, even as religious leaders, are among the first to deride, obstruct, undermine and attempt to prevent the Catholic education to the service of which you are dedicated.

It is important that we remember that if our friends are many, our enemies are far from few; and if their hatred is leveled at every aspect of Catholic life and thought, it is aimed with special fury at our schools.

This should not discourage you. Quite the contrary: it should inspire you to labor with ever greater love and zeal for the cause of Christ, the Divine Teacher Whose human aides you are.

Education for Christian Living

There is no possibility of devoting too much time and thought to the basic aims and principles which underlie our efforts in Catholic education. Pope Pius XI, in his encyclical on "The Christian Education of Youth," has perhaps summarized most succinctly the essence of Christian education:

> "The proper and immediate end of Christian education is to co-operate with Divine grace in the forming of the true and perfect Christian, that is, to form Christ Himself in those regenerated by baptism."

Such is your ideal, an ideal which often becomes obscure and appears unrealistic in the face of multiplying methodologies, techniques, the surrounding pagan environment, the materialistic goals of even the very young, and consequent fatigue and discouragement. The more exalted the ideal, the more we naturally tend to discouragement while working for its realization; but discouragement has no place in the Christian mentality. I suggest that the main reason for the existence of this paralyzing emotion lies in over-emphasis on working *for* Christ, and not enough emphasis on working *in* Christ. At the outset, then, let us recall a fundamental principle: God's purposes are eternal, and the power He gives us is beyond all calculation. That power is "Jesus Christ, and Him Crucified." His divine power works in and through our human weakness; His very life is transfused into us. When St. Paul said, "In Christ dwelleth all the fullness of the Godhead bodily, and in Him who is the head of all principality and power you have received of that fullness," he meant the words literally, and so you must receive them, else where will come the power necessary for fulfilling your vocation "to form Christ Himself in those regenerated by baptism?"

When the Holy Child "went to school" in the small house at Nazareth, He was indeed the first of many brethren to learn from other Marys and other Josephs. There He learned about His Father,

learned to praise Him in the inspired prayers of the
Psalms, delighted to walk with God in His youth
and to increase in knowledge through the Scriptures
and the beauty of His handiwork through all
creation. In the kind of family and school environment which we can only hope to reproduce in our
families and schools, He was taught the social and
family customs of His time; He learned the skills
necessary to earn a living, as well as how to conduct
Himself in society. In that first Christian school
basic patterns were established for generations to
come. Our age is no exception. Differences which
exist between our age and preceding centuries are
more apparent than real. Wars, corruption in
government, and all manner of sins were as prevalent then as they are now. Trace in memory the cries
of God's Prophets through the centuries before the
birth of Christ, and you will perceive that the invention of the hydrogen bomb has not essentially
modified human nature, even though it may modify
the face of the earth. Almost two thousand years
ago, in days not too different from our own, one
little boy and young man "went to school" as your
students do now. It is only truth to say that He is
still in school—in your school, for it is your task "to
form Christ Himself in those regenerated by
baptism."

Every child is a social being, destined to live
in society, to save his own soul and the souls of

others in society. To educate for full Christian living, then, is to educate for social living, and in particular for family life. In our day, when Christian
home life is so unhappily on the wane, it is of the
utmost urgency that we direct our attention and
energies to preparing students for family life *while
they are in school*. Where else will they learn to live
as later they will want to live, whether in the
religious families, or in families of their own? I wish
to suggest to you that education for Christian living
must be education for Christian family living. or it
is not, properly speaking, worthwhile education at
all. We sometimes forget this, and the students
themselves view their education as preparation for
making money, for a career, for "emancipation," for
anything except exactly what it is: twelve or sixteen
years of learning experiences in the supreme art of
that complete surrender to God through Christ
which is sanctity.

Let us consider what Christian family living is,
and how we can perhaps reproduce it within our
classrooms—at least in its main outlines.

First of all, any work or vocation whatever, is
a going to God through Christ, in faith, in hope, in
love. Family life is at once a personal and a social
or group way of going to God through Christ. It is
a finding of Christ in the family community, a loving of Christ with all one's powers of loving. It is
the vocation to know, love and serve Him in others,

where He actually lives and sleeps, works and eats, suffers and prays—in the members of the family. We recall that the early Fathers of the Church loved to refer to the family as "the little Church," because they so clearly perceived through faith that, just as He lives sacramentally in the Holy Eucharist, so by His indwelling He lives in each baptized soul as in His temple.

Family life anywhere, then, is a vocation to love, and its purgative and ascetic elements are reorganized in the fact that to love means to give rather than to receive, to receive in the very giving. To pass from self-love to Christ-love is the work of every life, and is the first lesson the child must learn in the course of his Catholic education.

In the second place: since Christian family living is group living, sacramental living, liturgical living, love-living and Christ-living, the school strives to bridge the gap too often existing between school and life, between altar and home.

It is the individual who comes haltingly to school, and he leaves, it is hoped, a member of the community of school life. He has learned group living as opposed to self-living, not because it is easier, or because society or etiquette demand it, but because this is the *Christian* way. He has been taught that the Christ who is the object of his growing knowledge and love is to be found in the very midst of the community which comprises his particular class, school, family. Christ is our great sacrament. School and family—these communities are in reality outward, visible signs of His inner, grace-bestowing Presence, His presence in His Mystical Body. Our students must be taught the happiness of finding and loving Christ in the school community, in each member of it. They will then be prepared intelligently to find and love Him in their family communities. Nor can we forget that such training is a necessary antidote against that prevalent habit of mind which views religion as subject to be learned and often forgotten, rather than as a Person to be learned and loved throughout life.

Christian family living is sacramental living. This means two things: participating ever more fully in the divine life of grace by frequent reception of the Sacraments; and sacramentalizing our daily lives. We must always be realistic. As realists, we see that Christian family living is not going on to any great extent in the midst of our secularistic environment. It almost seems at times that Christ is the most *un*important Person in the world, in America, on any street. To put Him in His first and proper place in the lives of students is something that we cannot do ourselves. The Catholic school may plant, the individual through her efforts may water, but it is God Who gives the increase. Through the Sacraments, those seven channels of grace, God gives, protects, increases and brings to fulfillment the Christ-life in every soul. The Sacraments are the chief instruments for living Christocentric lives.

What do we mean by sacramentalizing life? We come to a consideration of sacramentals, which have been called extensions of the Sacraments, because, like Sacraments, they are external rites which confer special spiritual benefits, though not directly as do the Sacraments. Sacramentals have their place in education and in Christian family living, for both of these are social areas in which individuals work together to restore all things in Christ. In the Catholic school, our students should become acquainted with the sacramentals, learn their place in Christian life, their uses, and become familiar with the relatively untapped mine of spiritual wealth which the Church offers us in them. People who live in the country desire the blessing of the Church on seeds, fruits, crops, eggs, butter, cheese. We ask God to bless the food we eat in His service.

So important are the sacramentals that the Church has extended and adapted them to the needs of the 20th century. Railroads, telegraphs, typewriters, printing presses, airplanes, seismographs, and countless other articles of daily life are blessed for our use, so that the baptized Christian will not suffer excessively from living in a pagan world. School experience in living with the help of sacramentals is training for Christian family living, for those days when our young women will rejoice

to have their homes and bridal chambers blessed,
when mothers will receive the Church's blessing
before and after childbirth in an intelligent and
loving fashion, and sign their children with holy
water before putting them to bed at night. Family
living and school living become Christian when everything in the home and school is consecrated to
God's service and used in His praise, to His greater
glory.

If the family is "a little church," it ought to
reflect daily the life of the larger Church, the Mystical Body of Christ. In fact, it is impossible to
separate the two. The Christian family is a cell of
that Body, and lives by its life. We often call this
living "liturgical living." How anxious each one of
you should be to help the students to appreciate the
fact that Our Lord lives in His Church, and more
fully in each soul as the soul lives with Him through
the liturgical year. Each mystery, each season, each
feast of the Church's year brings with it a particular
increase of grace, grace which becomes each student's, if he is brought into contact with the full
stream. There is no more secure way to a fuller life
in Christ than to follow the liturgical year in school
and home. We wish, therefore, to see each Catholic
school a place where the fullness of Christian living
is found, taught and lived. From altar to school
life—preferably with daily Mass beginning the

school day—and from altar to home life; this is the basic formula for Christian living, since Christ gives us His life from the altar.

Let us think briefly of this kind of living in school and home. First of all, the Church's new year begins with the First Sunday of Advent. If life has any meaning at all, that meaning does not rest in the fact that we are all simply *alive,* but rather, that we are living in Christ, and He in us. Advent is the time when your classes long once more for His three-fold coming: His coming at Christmas, His coming into each soul, and His final coming at the end of the world. During the prayerfully expectant days of Advent, it has become the custom in some schools to display a visible representation of this longing with the hanging of the Advent wreath in school and home.

We don't need advanced degrees in psychology to appreciate the educative importance of appropriate symbolism in the life of the child. Even the most sophisticated is impressed by the simplicity of the evergreens, symbolizing eternity; the four candles which represent the four weeks of expectation for the moment when we hear again, "Hodie," "Today," "Today a Child is born, the Expected of nations has come. . . ." How frequently parents wish that there was some way to assuage the disappointment which attends the discovery of their children that "There can't be a Santa Claus, because there

are too many boys and girls for him to get around to; and besides, we don't have a chimney." It will be a relief to parents as well as to their children to learn that the giving of Christmas presents, such a tedious and secular business at best, can be sanctified by recalling the original meaning of it all— the wish to imitate God's great love and generosity in giving His Son as our Redeemer.

Winter's drabness is lighted by the blessed candles of Candlemas day, which, with proper instruction, become more than gloomy reminders that on some gloomy day someone in the home may die, and are seen as reminders of the fact that, just as the child in spirit accompanies Mary to the temple bearing his blessed candle, so the candle teaches him that he is another Christ, an important person through whom Christ wishes to shine into the darkness of the world. Lent affords a splendid opportunity to do away with dull concepts centered about the duller prospect of "going without candy." It can be properly viewed by even the youngest child as the season of renewal for the whole Church, the Church's springtime, when every student shares in (not just remembers) the Passion and Death of Christ by his intelligent, informed self-denial, so that he may more fully share in His Easter Resurrection. During the Easter season of renewal and new life, Holy Mother Church consecrates all things to God again. There are blessings of water, food, bread, new fruits, and even of Easter eggs. At least some of these blessings should be carried into the life of the student, as a reminder that he, too, has risen to a new life in Christ. The presence of the Paschal candle from Easter to Ascension is a constant reminder of Christ, and of each child's baptismal vocation to radiate the Light of the World; while Pentecost is the occasion for recalling the first coming of the Holy Spirit to the Church, as well as His coming to each soul at Confirmation.

In addition to these mentioned days of light and grace in the liturgical year, there is the entire sanctoral cycle, as well as the special feastdays of each school, parish, family and child. The project of recalling students' baptismal days has been tried in some schools as a concrete way of putting first things first. By these devices, and many more, students learn through experience that this is the true life into which they were incorporated at Baptism—their life in Christ, as He lives again His life of praise, suffering, worship, prayer and redemption in His Body, the Church. We can only call such a program—Christian family life, whether lived in home or school.

Education for Christian family living is also education in what we may call "love-living", an art about which much is said today but little is known. Because every Christian family reproduces the Church in miniature, it is a community of love and sacrifice. These two arts, of love and sacrifice, are learned primarily in the great school of love, the Mass, where Christ, Who gave His life for us once historically, gives it daily until the end of time in each Mass. Right teaching about the Mass is probably the best method of insuring the realization of your principal goal as Catholic educators—education for sanctity. Youth requires and demands true concepts of its fundamental dignity. Students need and want to know: that they have been consecrated at baptism and strengthened by grace at Confirmation, in order to return God's love by their own total oblation to Him through Christ.

In a world dying of emptiness and starving on the husks of self-love you must continue to hold that standard of love and strength so lofty that only God Himself could have conceived it. The Mass is the greatest exchange of love between Christ and His Church, for every single soul. If we were to reduce the totality of Catholic education, everything you are striving to accomplish, to one single word, that word, I think, would be "love", that is, education in loving Christ or education in the Mass. And because people learn to love by loving, not by reading or hearing of it, it logically follows that the heart of every Catholic school ought to be the school of daily Mass. Difficulties toward the establishment of such a program abound; but if we weigh these apparent difficulties against the desired goal and the lofty means of achieving it, they are seen as problems which can often be solved simply by the will that they be solved.

In every Catholic school, the Mass should hold first place, not a something occasionally a part of academic life because it happens to be a *Catholic* school, but as something integral to it, the thing that *makes* it a Catholic school. We have remarked that family life on all levels and wherever lived is at once a personal and a social way of going to God. It has perhaps occurred to you that the same thing is true of the Mass: a personal way, because the individual gives himself; a social way, because the whole Christ, Head and members, is offered to God. St. Augustine summed it up in his masterful fashion when he said, in one of his sermons to his people: "If you are the Body of Christ, and His members, then that which is on the altar is the mystery of yourselves." Students who have learned how to love and how to sacrifice in the school of the Mass, will find that these arts are the same everywhere and throughout their lives; that the object of their love is always one, and the same: Christ Our Lord.

* * *

These few thoughts on the general nature of the training which will best fit your students for their destiny as saints are rooted in the great doctrines of the Incarnation and the Mystical Body.

These doctrines, when lived with faith, hope and love, have always served as the climate, the food, on which saints whom we revere today—and who also "went to school"—were nourished. They have not lost any of their sanctifying power and efficacy, but because only faith reveals them, they are often overlooked. It is one of the misfortunes of modern life that we are rather out of touch with quiet, unglamorous, apparently "getting nowhere" living, the kind of living that people today call "mediocre," or "humdrum." Blessed indeed by all students is the Catholic teacher who sees these doctrines through faith as absolutely the most exciting, real and worthwhile *facts* in life. Such a teacher is the *best* instructor of youth, for there is nothing quite as contagious and compelling as the fruits of such faith: peace, true fraternal affection, selflessness, spiritual joy. I urge each of you to regard it as your first work, to continue to grow in this kind of faith, hope and charity.

Yours is the heritage and example of Nazareth, of a centuries-old procession of educators who also labored "to form Christ Himself" in young people who flocked to monastic schools, to great universities, to one-room prairie schoolhouses. "They that instruct many unto justice shall shine as stars for all eternity"; but brighter and more resplendent yet will be the shining beauty of His Body, the Church, which Christ will present to His Father on the Last Day; that Body which you other Marys and Josephs have lovingly tended and cared for, as once was done in Nazareth.

If those who teach are not spiritual leaders, then they have missed the meaning of their calling, and society has few other places to turn.

The Lessons of St. Paul

Teaching is a difficult career. Like all leaders, teachers belong to the people, and their lives are lived in public. They share with other leaders the lack of privacy, proverbially called "of the goldfish bowl." Their faults are magnified and, many times, their very virtues are interpreted as faults by those who do not know how to evaluate them. Their pupils require unreasonable things of them. From the little tot in the kindergarten who complained that the teacher didn't seem to know very much because she put all the questions up to the class, to the college student who blames his own intellectual short-comings on the methods of this or that professor, the teacher is often asked to bear, along with his own burden, the burdens of others who should know how to lift their own.

Yet there are rewards and compensations which make the teacher content to disregard the drawbacks and forget the sacrifices. For teaching is a glorious career. Within its outer circumference stand the philosophers, the missionaries, all those who have advanced science and learning, all those who have reached out intellectually to their fellow men.

But today I am thinking of teaching in its narrower, technical aspect: I am thinking of those who preside in the classrooms of our common schools, those who from kindergarten to college prepare the next generation to take their place in society, to win their eternal reward. Teaching on this level is our most important profession because its services are fundamental. Upon the quality of primary and secondary education depend the excellence of our professions and the strength of our leadership.

The great men of all ages have concerned themselves either generally or particularly with education: some, like Confuscius, Aristotle and St. Thomas Aquinas, with the philosophy of education; some, like Plato and St. Jerome, with its content. Popes and bishops have legislated on the granting of licenses to teach. St. Paul, the most eminent teacher of them all, is our authority on the two great cardinal virtues of the teacher: patience and unselfishness.

I have no doubt but on the faculty of a school of education St. Paul would be giving courses on methodology and on the "personality of the teacher." And so well qualified would he be that I ask you to consider him with me, for in your New Testament reading his courses are available to you all. Let us examine, first, his qualifications for the position, that is, his education.

Saul, or Paul, had received an exemplary training. He had spent his youth in long, hard study. His knowledge of the civilization of which he was a part, of its history, its law, its customs was so profound and it had become so integrated with his desires and emotions, his will, his nature, his purpose of existence that when Our Lord came to fulfill the prophecies and change the customs and proclaim a new law, Saul, convinced of the righteousness of the Pharasaical position, went out to kill the followers of Christ, and we are introduced to him, a young man, guarding the cloaks of those who drove Stephen out of the city and stoned him to death. Had Saul not known how to weave his learning into the very fiber of his existence, had he not seen that knowledge cannot be a dull, inactive acquisition, but must become a live, impelling force, had he not realized that conviction and propagdana must go hand in hand, then St. Paul might never have become a vessel of honor and the object of the most dramatic and miraculously direct call to the service of God recorded by history.

"Saul, Saul, why dost thou persecute me?" And Saul, trembling and amazed, answered at once: "Lord, what wilt thou have me do?"

And what did Paul do? He went back to college, we might say. He had all his learning to reassess, all his values to redetermine, a whole new volume of theology to learn. He sought out those who had sat at the feet of Christ. From them Paul learned earnestly, eagerly, profoundly, effectively. He became the great writer of the new law, the great expounder of the new dispensation. Because of his knowledge of eastern Mediterranean cultures he knew how to apply the new theology, the new philosophy to the needs of the tottering societies to which he ministered. He knew how to teach the new law to the members of those societies, even as now, 2000 years later, he teaches it to us.

By nature, St. Paul was hot and impetuous, and not a well man, certainly not the type we should seek out as an exponent of that essential virtue which every teacher must possess if he would not fail as a teacher—the difficult virtue of patience. Yet read St. Paul's lessons and see how he sets forth the fundamental beliefs and practices of Christianity, taking one method of approach for the Israelite, another for the Hellenistic Jew, a third for the pagan Greek, presenting his matter now from one angle, now from another, over and over again. Always the master of patience. Even in his sorrow and indignation toward converts who had slipped back into the infidelities of heresy—always the master of calm and patient reasoning.

Whence came this virtue of patience to so impetuous a man? He tells us whence. It is of the essence of his charity. Charity, he wrote, is patient, is kind. Charity bears with all things, believes all things, hopes all things, endures all things. Indeed, these paragraphs of his First Epistle to the Corinthians might have been used as a preface to a treatise on methodology, had his first interest been in pedagogy.

I say, first interest, because it is clear that St. Paul had very real pedagogical interest: that he was a trainer of teachers. If you will think back into your knowledge of history of apostolic times, it will be patent to you that while St. Paul was instructing the Church of all ages in the fundamental importance and nature of charity, at the moment he was addressing his recently converted Christians not only as individuals but also as teachers. He was giving them the knowledge they must have as individuals in order to share in the fruits of the Redemption, and he was at the same time getting them ready to spread the new Faith among their Jewish and pagan neighbors. "Lord, what would you have me DO?" Even before his study of Christianity, Paul knew that religion was a social as well as an individual obligation. The Church, as Our Lord Himself told us, is a teaching body. "Go ye and teach" is its divine charter. The Christians to whom St. Paul was addressing his words on charity and on its by-product, patience, knew that they were dedicated to the apostolate because of the essential character of the Church as a teaching body. The Catholics of our century seem to be missing the knowledge which St. Paul's converts had: that when the missionary activity of a member of the Church is zero—missionary in the sense of helping his neighbor to know and appreciate the teachings of Christ—then that member of the Church has cut himself off from the very spark of the teaching body into which he has been baptized.

St. Paul goes on and tells his class in pedagogy more about charity. It is not ambitious. It does not seek its own—it is not self-seeking. Here is the secret. You do not seek your own advantage. You are exercised by the needs of others—that is to say, the needs of your students. You think of them, first, last, and really all the time. You do not permit yourself to be or become self-centered. Rather, in time, you discover the way to selflessness, in aim and devotion.

I am personally acquainted with many teachers who have learned this way and are trodding this road. Have they advanced professionally, perhaps you ask. I answer: they are at the top of their profession. They are its lights, its beacon lights. But what about their positions? Do they hold the positions which are called in the vernacular "the top jobs"? Well, as a matter of statistics, some of them do. I might be tempted to add "oddly enough," if I did not take literally the words of Christ: "Seek first the kingdom of God and His justice, and all these things shall be given you besides." Therefore, I am never surprised to find worldly success united to sacrifice and unselfishness.

In 1954 I lost in death a friend who was a great teacher, Miss Anna Kelley, of Peabody, Massachusetts. She was a pioneer in adult education, especially among aliens. She was one of two chosen officially in the entire country to go to Oxford University for specialized work in Basic English. The papers said of her, at the time of her death, that she never sought the limelight, even though she was recognized as without a peer in her field; that she was modest, and wholehearted in her devotion. As St. Paul put it, she did not seek her own advantage. In her last years, though her health was beginning to fail, she still found time for her neighbor and God's poor.

Among her acts of charity stands prominent the organization of the Aquinas League in Peabody, an organization of school personnel in the Archdiocese of Boston. Most of its members are from the public schools—but not all; most of them Catholic, but not all. There are sixty-seven different organizations in the Archdiocese, and it is still expanding. In each of its sixty-seven organizations, a very high percentage of Catholic teachers and a sprinkling of others teaching in the community belong—and it is still expanding. It is a strong and devoted affiliate to the Cardinal Cushing Charity Fund. I assign their contributions to help in my heavy budget for mentally ill children. The League came to me in a spirit of beautiful charity and utter good will and asked only that their contributions go directly to the carrying on of some good work, rather than to a building program. The League exemplifies the words of St. Paul: it is charity in action.

In Peabody, Miss Kelley not only organized the League but she remained its treasurer up to a few months before her death. Her power of leadership was unchallenged. She had all the time in the world for a labor of love. The basis of her success was charity. She lived the lessons of St. Paul.

The newspapers said that Anna Kelley was in a class by herself. Well, so she was, if we include in this phrase all those who love God and their fellow man enough to make the expression of that love a life work. I look around in the cities and towns of the Archdiocese and I see teachers by the score giving of their leisure, in fact, giving up their leisure, to helping others: teaching by their word and example the lessons of St. Paul on the teachings of Christ, rejoicing in the Truth. Society is leavened by these teachers and in turn they take back to the classroom knowledge and wisdom unattainable through any other mode of living.

Christ–Yesterday, Today, Forever

All truth, whatever its sources or subject matter, is ultimately from God. By His creative Hand
the laws were written, the natures determined and
the essences decreed which form the objects of
human research, scrutiny, study and science. His
Eternal Son is the Infinite Word which sums up all
the perfections and possibilities which admit of observation or speculation. All spoken wisdom, all
reasonings, all knowledge among men are but
broken reflections on His Infinite Truth, half-heard
echoes of His most perfect Wisdom. Even the pro-

fane sciences, even the most secular of studies
which have matter and the purely physical for
their object, even these speak to us of God and His
creative power and sovereign Providence. Indeed,
in order to *think* even of things most removed from
Him in nature and in dignity, we must use the faculties with which He has Himself endowed us, to
which He gave life and purpose and power.

All truth, whatever its source or subject matter, comes from God—and all the sciences, arts and
other disciplines depend on God for their origin,
their validity and the powers by which you know
them. Nature, no less than Revelation, is a book
through which God speaks to us and science, no less
than faith, though in a different way, brings us always back to God.

Christ, the Divine Teacher, Founder of the
Universal Church, taught another and higher form
of knowledge. "And I will ask the Father, and He
shall give you another Paraclete, that He may abide
with you forever. The spirit of truth, whom the
world cannot receive, because it seeth Him not,
nor knoweth Him: but you shall know Him; because He shall abide with you, and shall be in you."

This more sublime, more perfect knowledge
comes by Faith. A Catholic university must consider her mission unfulfilled if students leave the
campus with only the wisdom the world can give,
gleaned from the things the world can see and

know, the things that decay, disintegrate and die. The full work of a Catholic university has been done only when sense knowledge has been supplemented by Faith, and perfected by that Spirit of Truth Whom the world cannot receive, because it seeth Him not, nor knoweth Him. But you shall know Him for He shall abide with you and shall be in you.

By Faith, the spirit of truth, the "other Paraclete" which Christ promised, becomes diffused through your hearts. And thus by Faith there enters into the minds of men, otherwise at variance and contradictory to one another, a principle of unity and stability. Many and changing are the thoughts of men; the word of God is always the same. Fleeting and insecure is the knowledge based on purely human powers; steadfast and abiding is the knowledge based on divine Faith.

Because the Church is founded on Faith in the Eternal God, because she lives by her unfailing Faith and transmits the Faith unchanged down through the ages, the Church has become the principle of permanence in an insecure world, a divinely established rock firmly fixed among the shifting sands of human history. Nations, civilizations, theories, even philosophies—all these come, they have their little day, and they disappear. The Church abides.

The stability of the Church, her faithful witness to the eternal, unchanging God, should commend her to men of sound philosophy and of a truly scientific spirit. The most exalted minds of every age have pointed out how the infinite God must by His nature be above the ebb and flow of things created and finite. The mystic, the philosopher, the sensitive spirit of every thoughtful person, each recognizes that all else but God passes; God only endures. All forms of knowledge which have for their object created nature and things material are, like their objects, mutable; they not merely change but change is proper to their very nature. But religion, religious *faith*, should bear a constant witness. Its trumpet must sound no uncertain note. It sounds the same note in fair days that it does in foul, in the face of kings that it does in the ears of the poor, in prosperous lands as among the defeated and the destitute, in this century as it did in the centuries gone by. The object of Faith is God and God does not change. The channel of Faith is God's Incarnate Son and He is *yesterday* and *today* and *forever* the same.

Yet, many there are who resent the inflexible, unswerving permanence of the Faith and who deplore the uncompromising fidelity of the Church. Many there are who are offended by the stability of the Church and by her constant resistance to the demand that she, the unchanging witness to the

Eternal God, put aside her pretensions to permanence and descend into the arena of conflicting opinions and chaotic change. Many of those who are divided among themselves appear able to unite on one point and one point only: the demand that the Church abdicate the fixed convictions of her constant faith or else suffer the reproach of men who profess to be free, not to say the persecution of those who demand complicity in their confusion as the price of their friendship.

No small part of the malice currently fostered against the Church is due to resentment against her insistence on the divine rights of religious orthodoxy, on the necessity for unqualified and unchanging adherence, in letter and in spirit, to God's revelation of Himself through Christ *yesterday, today* and *forever* the same. Most of those who preach or write against the Church and who denounce the Faith as static or obscurantist and her leadership as reactionary and spiritual Fascism, would desist if the Church would come down from the exalted rostrum on which she bears her unchanging witness to God's Eternal Sovereignty and take her place in the confused mob of contending spokesmen for sectarian religion.

This is not the first period of history in which the Church has been condemned for her refusal to *change,* to accomodate herself to the religious, political, scientific and social moods of the hour.

I could describe in dramatic terms this ancient conflict between the spirit of truth and the spirit of error, between the Church of Christ and the partisans of spiritual compromise. I could tell you how one by one the succeeding generations have come to the doors of the Vatican, the citadel of the Christian Faith. They have knocked there with buskin and with boot, with pikes in their day and later with rifles, and sometimes with the swagger sticks of diplomacy. Each time the Faith has appeared under the frail and wasted form of a high priest, usually an old pope of three score years and ten or more. Even to the world he is a symbol of all his kind, of all Christ's priesthood and of all who share his Faith. But he is more than a symbol—he is the secret of constancy, the source of confidence, the cornerstone of indestructible Faith.

To the emissaries of compromise and of change who stand by her gates, the Church, through the lips of some old pontiff, always asked: "What do you desire of me?"

"We ask you to *change* . . ."

No less constant is the answer: "I can never change!"

But everything changes in this world. Politics change, science changes. Medicine has changed. Philosophy has changed. All things human change. Why must *you* remain always the same?

"Because I come from God. I speak for God. I am answerable to God. And God is always the same."

Then in each generation the particular emphasis varies, but the basic challenge is this: All this pertains to another order of things—to the world beyond, perhaps. But now you are in *our* world. Here below *we* are the masters and here in the world you are answerable to us—to us, the Emperors of the Roman State who oppress you in Clement and Calixtus and Marcellus the martyrs; and to me, Attila the Hun, Scourge of God, who threatened you in Leo, the Saint; to us, the German kings who defy you in Pope St. Gregory and the French absolutists who harass you in Pope Boniface; to me, Napoleon who holds you captive in Pius VII; to us, the prophets of the new nationalism who mock you in Pius IX and Leo XIII; to us, the founders of the new philosophy and the proud agnosticism who despise you in Pius X; to us, the *duces,* the *fuehrers,* the *marshalls,* and the *commissars,* who revile and defraud you in Pius XI, and Pius XII; to use the spellbinders of the new psuedo-democratic secularism who propose to cripple your mission and scatter your people. On earth you are answerable to us—to our Atheism, Secularism, Statism, Nationalism, Militarism, Racism, Communism, whatever form the system behind our demand may take. We have millions of men under arms. We shall draw the sword. The sword which can topple thrones and decimate nations is well able to slash the pages of inspired Scriptures and ecclesiastical encyclicals.

The Church replies: Blood yields the aroma in which I inevitably recover my youthful vigor. Martyrdom restores my pristine innocence and strength. Persecution is the instrument of my purging and renewal! I shall render to Caesar the things that are Caesar's and to God the things that are God's. On Peter, the Rock, I was built and the gates of hell shall not prevail against me.

That same spirit of God which guarantees the stability of the Church is present in *you*. Christ has sent His other Paraclete to abide in *you*. You *are* the Church and all *her* characteristics should be *yours*.

Let her Faith within you be the *permanent* element in your lives—the stable principle underlying all your mental and cultural and spiritual growth. Stand fast in that Faith and then you can keep your minds open to wholesome change in all other things of which change is the law. Then can you take your place, as take your place you should, in the vanguard of every movement which seeks to reinterpret, to revise or even to revolutionize the service of men. But stand fast, I adjure you, in the Faith that you have received through the apostles from the Christ Who speaks for God.

So long as you abide in the Faith, you will be the hope of the world and the instruments through which the Church gives the world her greatest service. Through you, the Church will fulfill her great social mission among men: to be the principle of permanence in a world of change; the wellspring of sanctity in the midst of evil; the beacon of idealism in an age of cynicism and of the crudity which passes for realism; a ground for hope in the face of discouragement and mounting fear.

"To Form Jesus Christ Himself..."

"I think I am losing my Faith since I came to this Catholic college. When I was younger, in high school and in the Service, I knew God; but now I only know innumerable facts about Him. What is happening to me?"

"This month we have started to study the Sacraments. I can scarcely remain in class—it is so sterile. Must theology be lacking in joy, enthusiasm, vitality?"

"What is wrong with this college? Nothing I learn helps me to live a better Christian life. No one here really believes that faith is greater than anything else, that grace is more powerful than a dollar bill."

"Let's face it, fellows: the jobs we get later on will destroy our capacity to be human. We won't be able in later years to meditate, to pray, to contemplate. It's part of living in a technological age. If I ask my parents how to live a Christian life in such an age, they do not understand the problem; if I ask a priest, he says: 'Go to the Seminary'; if I ask our profs they say, 'It is the problem of our times.' Isn't there any answer?"

These are exact quotations of questions asked by students in a Catholic college. Were they asked on your campus? I should like to ponder the problems which confront those of you who have the tremendous responsibility of educating today's sensitive, thoughtful, and often discouraged youth.

It is such an easy matter, such a human thing, to persuade ourselves that all is well, or to dismiss such students as immature, malcontents, or neurotic. It is such an easy matter to forget fundamentals in the press of daily administrative tasks. Even were we to know that such students are immature or bewildered; yet the thoughts, the searchings, the bewilderment of youth can be so clear-sighted, so penetrating, so unclouded by the exigencies of life which will later face them, that to disregard their words is to disregard the clearest light that will ever

shine into the complexities and dimmer lights of the
mature mind. Our colleges exist to answer these
questions, for the task of education through the
centuries has always been to answer the needs of
man in the age in which he lives. Yours is a sublime
vocation, an awesome responsibility: "To form Jesus
Christ Himself in those regenerated by Baptism."
We do not have to ask whether the students think
this challenge is being met; we simply have to open
our eyes and see that it is not always being
fully met.

I am keenly aware of the burdens you bear
with such constant courage and fortitude: the burdens of retaining in its vitality the heritage of
liberal education in a scientific era; burdens which
are heavily financial, involving as they do problems
of survival and expansion—with little or no surplus
for either. I am equally aware of the necessary burden of constant reassessment and re-evaluation of
the academic status of our institutions of higher
learning. Reassessment involves demonstrating a-
gain and again the relevancy of the liberal arts
tradition in the modern world. Re-evaluation concerns itself with those increased areas of contemporary knowledge and specialization which challenge the liberal arts curriculum: what should we
assimilate, and what cannot be dispensed with?
The struggle to maintain the tradition of humanism
in a century which must, to young eyes, seem the

antithesis of the human is inevitably related to problems financial and academic.

Yet I view these problems, grave though they are, as secondary, for the primary purpose of Catholic education on every level is "to form Jesus Christ Himself in those regenerated by Baptism."

It is the specific function of the college and the university to train the intellectually mature adult so that he will become capable of rendering service to God directly and through the community at large; but unless our foundation is deeper and our purpose more sublime, in what do we differ from nonsectarian colleges? Our graduates must not be judged as successful products of the Catholic educational system solely on the basis of their reputations in business, scholarship and society; nor by the size of their homes and bank accounts. The intellectually mature adult, by reason of his training, may acquire these goods as accidents; but the judgmental norm is inevitably related to the primary purpose "to form the *supernatural* man, who thinks, judges and acts consistently in accordance with right reason, illumined by the supernatural light of the example and teachings of Christ." In the light of this aim the only proper norms are these: How *other* worldly are our graduates? *How much are they men and women of Faith?* How dynamic? To what degree are they not merely in possession of knowledge, but possessed by the source of Truth and Life, God Himself? To say it another way, to what extent in their lives does Christ Himself control, originate, motivate and dominate their every choice and every hour? For, is not this very outcome the logical consequence in a person in whom Jesus Christ Himself has been formed?

In the training of the college and university student, responsibility cannot be delegated to the home or to society. These students of yours are young adults, able to marry, to maintain a home, to serve in war, to perform the tasks of men and women. By their own testimony, they come to you to acquire the learning and skills necessary in order to live the better life. How do they define the "better life"? A generation whose entire life span has been dominated by the shadow of wars and rumors of war, many of whom bear on their bodies and in their souls the price of the peace we presently enjoy, does not equate the better life with three cars in every garage, and does not seek the easy way out. This young generation, which has never known the normal climate of a world at peace, is willing to sacrifice, but unwilling to endure the meaningless, whether it be the meaningless sacrifice or the meaningless life. The good life to them means the real, the true, the hard and sacrificial way willingly embraced in pursuit of reality. The problem of *meaning*, not of money or fame, is the problem with which your students are wrestling in the citadel of their souls. Suffering has this effect on individuals and on nations; it is God's purgative instrument. I can truly assert, therefore, that God's hour is at hand; more, that it is in your hands.

How often have we not heard: "This is the age of the laity"? Tremendous spiritual currents are generating the world over and throughout our own cherished land. For years now we have witnessed the spectacle of the Holy Spirit working almost visibly in the souls of men, engendering this divine discontent with anything less than full reality. In our own Archdiocese we have been blessed by an extraordinary degree of charity: churches, orphanages, hospitals and new schools are its external fruits. In the intellectual order, what years ago was only academically mentioned is now a byword: theology, with philosophy as handmaid, must be the unifying force of the college curriculum. In the spiritual order, time prohibits a recitation of the marvels of divine grace at work in such movements as the Family Apostolate, the development of the Catholic publishing field, and liturgical integration . . . to name but a few.

These marvelous and varied trends are manifestations of the problem of meaning in modern society, of man's dissatisfaction with unreality, of his hunger and thirst for an intimate, informed, intelligent union with God in his daily life. It is to this thirst to which Catholic colleges and universities must at all times and in all subject matter address themselves. Unless it be satisfied, we can reasonably predict that God's hour will pass, that men will faint on the way, that the Church in the United States will have built well in marble and stone, but less than well with the living cells which comprise the visible Body of Christ.

"To form Jesus Christ Himself in those regenerated by Baptism." What heroic efforts have been expended on this task! Men and women have given their very lives for it, both in religious life and in complete dedication to God in the world. Colleges stand and are being erected; the best minds in the Church have labored long years in study for their educative vocation. Yet youth asks: "What is wrong with this college? Nothing I learn helps me to live a better Christian life today." Perhaps the key we are searching for lies in the one word: *today*.

Does the college address its labors to answering the spiritual needs of man in the world *today?* Are its faculty members conversant with the problems of students *today?* We can never forget that students are also the products of their environment. The very first task in the life of every educator is to know the environment which has formed his students, to endure in his own spirit its bitterness, the anguish of its restless emptiness, the death of its dislocation, distortion, and lack of humanism. It is in the world of today that your students will pass the last two-thirds of their mortal lives. In it they will continue the search for the better life, suffer from its disintegration, and experience the death of lesser visions so that Christ may fully possess their lives. Their present questions and searching are the expression of their initial sufferings, and of their deepest fears and hopes.

For men of past generations and centuries which we call "the ages of Faith," "a Christian culture," and "a less complex world," the business of living was spiritually and psychologically a simpler matter than it is today. National customs, rooted in centuries of Catholicism, visibly enfolded them from the cradle to the grave in known, smaller, more stable boundaries. Their environment spoke to them of God in the way the Creator intended His creatures to learn: by immediate appeals to their bodies and their emotions, as well as to their intellects and wills. Life itself was a kind of universal classroom, and certainly it was a sacramental reality perceived. Today, on the other hand, the Church is engaged in a worldwide effort to speak in a non-human age to human beings in a language at once human and divine. Today the Author of human nature works through the Church, and through you as members of His Mystical Body to satisfy the hungers and thirst of your students in a universe, a society, and an environment almost new in human history. The truth remains unaltered, the message is the same, but it is taught to men who are products of an altered and a new environment. Therefore, educators must experience the essence of this new world in their own souls, and bear its sufferings in their spirits, as Christ Himself took on the sufferings of the human race in soul and body before He offered His life to redeem mankind. Indeed, it is Christ Himself Who continues His redemptive suffering in the souls of each one of you.

To enter into the spirit of modern man is to step into the exterior darkness of a non-Christian environment. Students of this generation are not fully children of the Light; for them the Light of God shines in a darkness which they cannot understand, and often It is quite invisible. "The Light shineth in the darkness, and the darkness does not comprehend it," wrote St. John sadly; but for men of good will we can interpret these words in a triumphant vein. The Light of God still shines upon the heart of the darkness of man's making; the journey of modern man into the radiance of His Light leads, in faith, into the very heart of darkness, to triumphant vision. Students must be told that the contemporary environment of exterior darkness caused by man's departure from God has operated to create in countless souls an interior darkness, the characteristics of which are those psychic and spiritual pains always inseparably connected with a lack of right order, a distortion of values, a wrenching of man's spirit attendant upon being unfulfilled. But these truths can be imparted with the authentic note of conviction only by those of you who have had compassion (in the etymological sense of the word) on the multitudes who present themselves year after year in your classes.

In thinking of these things, I recall the universal dismay of childhood before the unalterable fact of Humpty Dumpty's shattered state. You remember—that when Humpty Dumpty fell from his nursery rhyme wall, "not all the king's horses, and not all the king's men, could put Humpty Dumpty together again." The non-Christian environment is somewhat like Humpty Dumpty after his fall; it is the ages of Faith irrevocably shattered. For some years now many words have been spoken on the subject of how to put this world together again, and this has even been considered to be the work of the alert and dedicated Christian, the particular apostolate for which recent generations of our college students have hopefully been prepared. Perhaps the perplexity of this generation of collegians is the reflection of the dismay of childhood before the unalterable fact of Humpty Dumpty's shattered state. Can it really be done this way? There are many individuals who think not.

The search for God, the surrender to the love of God which constitute man's vocation in this life, must now be carried on in a manner evolving from the modern scene itself, and for this vocation your students must receive mature, realistic training. This vocation requires a journeying past the exterior shadows and its desolation into the very heart of spiritual darkness, the emptiness of the modern soul. There the man of faith is called to stand firm; to guard the faith, to motivate his hope and love by the faith of a St. Paul. "Custode fidem" Paul wrote to Timothy. Possessed by the redemptive Christ, encompassed by His peace, the student of faith must win again the mercy of God like the prophet of old. Let your students learn this fact from every professor who is first living it, from every course in the curriculum, from every religious exercise: God *can* be found in the technological age; God wills to be found by faith in the darkness which enfolds Him. There His love will continue to purify souls so that they will love Him alone as He suffers in His Body the Church to remake this shattered world.

This is the work of God Himself, but He looks to you, His human instruments, to instruct, to lead, to inspire, to encourage. The entire educative process ought to prepare the soul for the vision of God and the love of God which are the reason for man's creation and the fulfillment of his being. This requires, in the first place, a preparation for the perception of reality on the human and supernatural levels. Loss of the power to apprehend symbolic values, loss of contact with basically human elements in nature and in life, and the frenzied tempo of modern society must yield, slowly but surely, to what may be termed the contemplative habit of mind. These disciplines are necessary before man can become fully human again, able to hear the voice of the Spirit of God, able to perceive the meaning of the Sacraments, of every man, of created objects, of life itself.

The simplest things in life are often the hardest to see, especially for an age blinded by complexity. Teach your students that, although they were born into the exterior darkness of their century, each one must decide for himself whether he will remain there to die, or move on the strength of a willed and vibrant faith into the glorious night where the redemptive Christ awaits him. In this essential and solely necessary work of their lives they are nourished and strengthened, through the Holy Sacrifice of the Mass, the Sacraments, by prayerful union with the annually celebrated mysteries of our redemption, by the living, personal, and vital Christ Whom they seek.

Our present considerations are intimately related to Advent darkness and Advent longings. It was through the "Fiat" of the Virgin Mary that the

Divine Life of God shone in the darkness and became a reality to men in the Person of her Son. The
Book of Wisdom declares: "When all things are in
quiet silence and the night is in the midst of her
course, God's almighty word leaps down from
heaven . . . into the midst of the land of destruction."
There is no need to labor the obvious comparison
between the common destruction which lay over the
land of that first coming and the contemporary
scene. "His mercy is from generation unto generation, to those who fear Him"—so speaks the wait-
ing Mother of the Whole Christ. "With the coming
of the birthday of the Redeemer, our Holy Mother
the Church would bring us to the cave of Bethlehem
and there teach us that we must be born again and
undergo a complete reformation; that will only hap-
pen when we are intimately and vitally united to
the Word of God made man and participate in His
Divine Nature, to which we have been elevated."
(*Mediator Dei.*)

I pray for you and your students the fullness
of Mary's *faith* and Fiat, that through you the Light
of God will shine in the darkness of the modern
world in an endless incarnation.

The Heritage of the West

The urgency of the times makes it imperative for us to take counsel, to sharpen our thought in regard to the specific ideals for which we stand. This is a period of transition, of realignment. We are seemingly at the end of a civilization.

In a like period of history Saint Augustine remarked that of the liberal arts, only history, so far as it relates the truth, is worth knowing. Augustine was watching the death throes of the glory that was Greece and the grandeur that was Rome, and all the while, he was surrounded by pagans shouting that the desertion of the gods by the Christians was the cause of all the trouble. To repel the charge he wrote *The City of God*. It was the genius of Augustine to sift the loftiest, the finest, the best in the failing Graeco-Roman civilization, to Christianize it, and thus contribute to the classic, Christian, cultural heritage that is the basis of Western civilization and of Catholic education.

Western civilization is frequently presented as synonymous with the American Way of Life, a spiritual structure, a structure of ideas and ideals, of aspirations and values, of beliefs and standards, a synthesis of all that commends itself to the American as the right, the good, and the true in actual life.

If the American Way of life had to be defined in one word, "democracy" would undoubtedly be the word, but democracy in a definite American sense. On its political side it means the Constitution; on its economic side, "free enterprise"; on its social side, an equalitarianism; on its spiritual side, "idealism."

Western culture is obviously broader and deeper than this. It is the Graeco-Roman Tradition of literature and language, of philosophy, of architecture and art, of law and political concepts—monarchy, aristocracy, democracy. It is the super-imposed Judeao-Christian tradition of fructifying spirituality and ethics, of enriching their permeating influence on personal and social behavior, of emphasizing the distinction between the individual and the race, between liberty and authority, between mercy and justice, between what is Caesar's and what is God's. Such in broad outlines are the combination of factors that make up our Western civilization.

The part played by the Church in Western culture has been determinative and decisive. From the date of Christ's birth in Palestine the course of civilization has been so radically changed that we call it the Christian Era. After bitter persecutions the infant Church demonstrated its right to existence. Its growth in numbers was only outdistanced by its tremendous transformation in the thinking and conduct of men. The worship of many gods and goddesses of Western culture was forever forgotten: the importance of the individual, the value of human life, the sanctity of marriage, the glory of womanhood, the rights of nations all received an entirely new meaning. For the first time in history here was a religion that not only proposed the highest and most admirable ideals, but actually influenced in everyday practice the conduct of men's lives. And this not for an epoch or a century—it has grown and flourished and perennially springs into fresh vigor at every age.

At the birth of Christ the world was governed by oriental and Roman despots. Religion was purely formal, a worship of many gods and goddesses, who

had worse vices than men. The idea of the after-
life was pessimistic; for the Roman it meant a cheer-
less existence on some star, or in the nether regions.
To all this Christ gave the first heart-warming answers: One living God, the three Persons in the
Trinity, Divine Providence, the Creation, the fall
and Redemption of mankind, the establishment of
the Church, the sacrifice of the Mass, the sacraments, grace, heaven. This was profound enough
for the wisest and clear enough for the most un-
learned; it was satisfying because while it held up
high ideals, they were able to be lived and accomplished. The idea that this world was not the end
of life but the beginning, made understandable the
poverty and injustice of this world. It was the first
religion that could be lived, and fulfill the highest
aspirations of the human heart.

Socially the Church reformed the whole idea
of the Roman world: man was but a cog of the state,
women had fallen to a very low state, children were
liable to exposure if malformed, slaves were human
chattels; to all of this Christianity preached the eternal value of the individual, his immortal soul for
which Christ died, his rights which were independ-
ent of the state and which could not be taken from
him. Womanhood in the person of Christ's mother
now assumed the glory and partnership of marriage,
the heavenly trust of children and their formation
in the pattern of Christ. The protection of slaves

and their equality with all men before God and in eternal salvation—all these teachings gradually found their way into law, which we now take for granted.

It was the Church who reassembled the crumbling law and order of the Roman Empire, and presented to the world the only unifying and stabilizing force of peace and justice through the darkness of the barbarian invasions. She absorbed and christianized unnumbered hordes when Western civilization almost ceased to exist. It was her scholars who preserved the contributions of the Graeco-Roman world: the dramas of Athens, the philosophy and political theory of Plato and Aristotle, the history of Herodotus and Thucydides, the glorious architecture of Greece, Roman Law, administration and literature; the Church Christianized the whole of it into one living Faith and culture of the Middle Ages down to modern times.

In philosophy it was the genius of Augustine, Thomas, Bonaventure that adapted Greek philosophy into the modern complete system that we use today. It was St. Thomas who said that freedom, liberty, was the power to do what is right—not as some modern philosophers say, the power to do what is wrong; it was St. Thomas who said that law was a norm of reason in accord with God's law—not as some modern lawyers say, law is the will of the majority; it was St. Thomas who said that the state is subject to the law of God—not, as dictators say, that the state is superior to all law.

The Middle Ages are supposed to be the age of the Catholic Church, and hence backward and dark; but we owe more to the Middle Ages than to modern times: it was from the Middle Ages that we received our first constitutions and guarantees of individual liberties, that the king was subject to law; it is there that we find the origin of juries and writ of "habeas corpus," our parliaments and legislatures, our codes of law; in economics the theory that goods must be well made and sold for a fair price, that money was a secondary consideration, that our main object in life was our spiritual welfare, not our increased bank account. In education the early monastic and cathedral schools blossomed into the classic curriculum of arithmetic, geometry, music, astronomy, grammar, rhetoric, logic and the monumental universities of Paris, Bologna, Salerno, Salamanca, Louvain, Oxford, Cambridge. So too the art, sculpture, paintings of Giotto, Fra Angelico, Botticelli, Michelangelo, Leonardo da Vinci, Raphael, Titian, Correggio, all masters and all Catholic in thought and composition. The Dominican, Albert the Great, and the Franciscan, Roger Bacon, were only the first of a long line of Catholic scientists. Modern drama and music received their impetus and inspiration from church-sponsored plays and psalmody. The literature of the Middle Ages is full and classic: Dante's *Divine Comedy*; Chaucer's *Canterbury Tales*, the *Quest of the Holy Grail*, the poetry of the troubadors, the hymns of Benediction written by St. Thomas, the Dies Irae, the Stabat Mater, the *Confessions* and *City of God* by St. Augustine. Later ascetical writing is represented by St. Teresa of Avila, the Spiritual Exercises of St. Ignatius, St. John of the Cross, St. Francis de Sales. The very letters that we see on every page of print were developed in the time of Charlemagne; movable type, printing, first saw light in the book of books, the Bible.

And the Gothic Cathedrals! Notre Dame, Chartres, Rheims, Cologne, Canterbury and Lincoln. They were triumphs of architectural engineering and decorative art, but they were something more than this. Everything in them lifted the soul heavenwards. The soaring spires, the mighty pointed arches, exalted the worshipper to the very throne of God: "The painted glass, the statuary, the noble proportions were designed and understood to set forth the Christian altar, the worship and teaching of the Catholic Church." The Gothic cathedral was the monument of the ideals and aspirations not of a section of society but of society as a whole: "It stood not for a fragment of the life of a few devout people, but for a life in which all men of that time had a place." The divine worship of the cathedral "was regarded as the normal and natural develop-

ment of a man's life . . . The art of the cathedral told
men of the beauty and the springtime of that great
supernatural life which all men then believed to be
their heritage."

Concern for social welfare and labor has been
synonymous with the Church throughout all ages.
The hospitals, care of orphans, the aged were
throughout the Middle Ages the sole charge of the
Church. In modern times it was Leo XIII who
wrote the charter of the workingman, pronouncing
his right to organize, to a just wage, to proper living
and working conditions; all the things we associate
with labor unions, Leo XIII enunciated long before
they were born, and Pius XI and XII, and John
XXIII have kept the Church's teaching up-to-date
on social welfare, marriage, education, philosophy
and science.

Surely the Church has at all times deserved
well of history. Her contributions to the religious,
social, economic and cultural progress of the world
has been and is of the first importance. In philosophy, education, art, architecture, music, law and
political science, the Church has furnished the basis
of Western civilization. With the Revolt of the 16th
Century much of the main-stream of thought has
been diverted from the classic tradition; it is now
secular in thought and expression. No longer is
there one common creed, one ritual, one worship,
one sacred language, one Church, a single code of

manners, a uniform scheme of society, a common system of education, an accepted style of beauty, a universal art, a recognized standard of the good, the beautiful, and the true. But what is best and most enduring of our Western civilization, and particularly in our democratic system, derives from Christian ideals and ideas.

This is our heritage, our culture, our civilization. This is the historical background of the system of education that we represent. It aims today as always to make students realize that they are not merely *natural* creatures, but persons who possess a *supernatural* destiny; to develop the full range of all their capacities *supernatural* as well as natural; to train their intellects by the study of Divine Revelation as well as of human sciences and the arts; to train their wills in the service and love of God in obedience alike to the law of nature and to the higher law of grace; to love and serve their neighbors not only as fellow citizens, but as fellow creatures of God, and brothers in Christ.

Catholic Education is defending and preserving these deep spiritual values and traditions which secular civilization has lost. It is the one organ by which these essential truths can be related to modern culture on the intellectual plane and reintegrated with it by your patient efforts. No work is greater than this. None offers more creative possibilities for the future. And it is yours. Be proud of its background in divine revelation and human science and rejoice in its accomplishments throughout the ages. We are not called to chant the De Profundis over a glorious past. We are the heralds of the future for the restoration of all things in Christ. We are not called to gather the harvest but to sow the seeds of what was great and good throughout the ages and what is new and true in the present. May God be with you in the fulfillment of that exalted mission.

The Challenge

of Christian Education

In today's world, headlines scream about scientific advances and our race with the Soviets for missile supremacy, but thoughtful people are realizing that the battlefield in any "cold" or "hot" war will be the intellect of man. Opposing armies in today's battle represent opposing philosophies.

As early as 1899, John Ireland, Archbishop of St. Paul, warned: "This is an intellectual age. It worships intellect. It tries all things by the touch-

111

stone of intellect ... The Church herself will be judged by the standard of intellect. Catholics must excel in religious knowledge ... They must be in the foreground of intellectual movements of all kinds. The age will not take kindly to religious knowledge separated from secular knowledge."

Russell Kirk, a contemporary philosopher, speaking at Boston College in 1955, noted: "Despite all the predictions of the optimistic intellectuals of the past two centuries, most of the world now is back in the plight of the world of Father Edmund Campion, (the Jesuit martyr), and there will have to be many martyrs of Campions's cast, I think, before truth and justice may prevail again. The time is out of joint, and the cause of the present discontents ... is the ascendancy of intellectual errors."

Education seeks to draw out the elements of our common human nature. Men are the same and, therefore, the core of our education must be the same. Only the details will vary. Truth is one. Therefore, education should be basically one. The medieval world worked out this oneness with philosophy as the principle of order and theology as the principle of unity.

With the rise of relativism, however, the idea that schools exist in order to communicate truth has been diminished. If we divorce ourselves from the past in this manner, teachers must look around for an excuse for their own existence. Fads in American education have arisen because many Americans have been looking for reasons for the existence of American schools.

Naturalists in the educational world today preach that the aim of education consists of assisting the student to adjust to life, to society and to vocation. The Christian humanist answers: Schools exist to assist souls in attaining intellectual and moral perfection. On both supernatural and natural levels, we train young people to discipline themselves both mentally and morally. This process is not a mere "conditioning" of students, for such a mechanistic approach makes young people no more important than the dog in the famous conditioned-reflex experiment of Pavlov. Our answer lies, however, in a stable curriculum of liberal arts, or general education, as ordered by philosophy and unified by theology.

Honorable William Benton, a former Senator, concluded after some time spent in Russia studying the educational system of the Soviets: "We must abandon pragmatic-instrumentalism and return to a deep faith in a man as the son of God, and in the values which accrue to that status."

Looking into the future frightens some people for they see the possibility of man destroying himself as a result of his own scientific prowess. The

spectacular success of science in the development
and control of nuclear fission has inspired in educational circles a new respect for scientific study.
Such advances have made some men aware of the
truly magnificent gifts which God gave to man by
endowing him with an intellect and will. Great intellectual accomplishments stand always as a tribute
to the infinite knowledge and power of a Divine
Creator.

Our future, therefore, cannot be separated
from a program of scientific advancement. We have
already committed ourselves to such development
by investing billions of dollars into planned scientific development. This is the future confronting
Catholic educators.

We must realize, however, that education has
become a main theater of the cold war; Russia's
classrooms and libraries, her laboratories and teaching methods may threaten us much more than her
hydrogen bombs or guided missiles.

Along with the teachings of Holy Scripture,
some of the outstanding exemplars of our culture
include St. Athanasius, St. Augustine, St. Gregory
Nazianzen, St. Thomas Aquinas, St. Bonaventure,
St. Robert Bellarmine, and Suarez. Catholic education must face the challenge of the future armed
with these traditions of the past. Modern Christian
thought is seen through the background of our
Catholic Faith.

Our culture has grown from Judaic-Christian roots and from our Graeco-Roman background. A dark age in history is a period when a culture does not respond to its cultural roots. During the historic "Dark Ages," men turned their backs on their Graeco-Roman heritage.

Today we are in the midst of another "Dark Age." In modern education our Judaic-Christian roots are often ignored. The Old Testament tradition is left out of most history textbooks. Rather, Christ seems to appear out of the East bent on destroying Greek and Roman thought. A religious framework is missing from this world view. Our only hope lies in a Renaissance here. (William G. Pollard, *A Christian Idea of Education.*)

The restoration of a classical heritage would be useless without a spiritual foundation, however. Christian tradition should occupy the position the Graeco-Roman tradition of the past had—humanism as transmitted and transmuted by the Church.

Historically the decline of virtue in Roman education began when the art of oratory was sought without the philosophy of oratory. In the Middle Ages, too, scholastic argumentation and syllogistic reasoning often degraded into a formal exercise without the desire for Truth. The art declined because it was divorced from its purpose. Today the act of learning has degraded, in some areas, into a pseudo-science of how to teach. Many people do not contemplate seriously the purposes of this education.

Educational goals were shifted by the seventeenth century in America as the schools became permeated with the philosophy of puritanism. Even later, throughout the eighteenth century, a philosophical movement, inspired by the spirit of the Enlightenment, represented a reaction against the traditional philosophy and theology of Europe. These ideas which urged man to advance by means of unaided reason resulted in a spirit of liberalism which influenced the philosophy of America. We live with these results today in the form of rationalism and secularism.

Do parents really want to have their children exposed to a neutrality of such ideas in the classroom? Or do many parents really desire, along with the great Cardinal Newman, that their children's intellects receive the best training possible through definition, discussion, and debate about ideas?

Jacques Maritain, in *Education at the Crossroads*, has reminded us that "... the chief task of education is to shape man, or to guide the evolving dynamism through which man forms himself as a man. Man is not merely an animal of nature, like a skylark or a bear. He is also an animal of culture, whose race can subsist only within the development of society and civilization: he is a historical animal;

hence the multiplicity of cultural or ethico-historical patterns into which man is diversified; hence, too, the essential importance of education."

Thus, education involves that transmission of an inheritance, a culture and a creed. Education implies tradition, good or bad; it is passing on something. Schools should give what young people need in order to be the kind of person one should become. Schools are not mere service stations, providing what the students want. They must instead aim to cooperate with divine grace in forming true and perfect Christians, who will think, judge, and act as Christ would in our society.

Man is better than mere things. Our objective, therefore, is to develop a person, as a person, instead of merely teaching him to be a worker. He never loses his unique personality because of the mark which having an immortal soul lends to an individual. Our curriculum must put us in touch with this intellectual adventure of man—it must contribute to understanding and wisdom instead of to knowledge alone.

Having said these things, what shall we say about the particular problems which face us in planning for the future? Are these problems peculiar to Catholic educators?

All teachers could tell me about problems! They face problems day after day in the classroom. My problems are mostly administrative and pastoral. Only occasionally do I come into contact with the soul of a gifted child in the fifth grade. Exceptional children—dear to my own heart—are placed in the care of dedicated and trained individuals. You must live with these challenges daily.

The challenges of tomorrow, however, will face both the individual teacher, priest, and prelate. Foremost, of course, is the problem of sheer numbers. Along with population increases, the Church must provide for the large numbers of young people demanding higher education. Our colleges are bulging now and these institutions are wondering how to handle the expected increase in student enrollments within the next decades.

Numerical increases, of course, sometimes exert pressure which might result in a lowering of standards. All schools must answer this challenge, but Catholic institutions, especially, must meet this problem for we are committed to a system of education that begins and ends with God.

Apathy is one of our greatest enemies. Children are being graduated from high school with no real knowledge of the inherent evils of Communism. Can these young people fight something which is not clear to them? Only when we show the insidious nature of the doctrine which destroys man's freedom and attempts to destroy his belief in Almighty God, will we produce men and women who will sacrifice in order to protect their human rights.

Our work is clear. Education ought to teach us how to be in love always and what to be in love with. The great things of history have been done by the great lovers, by the saints and men of science and artists; and the problem of civilization is to give every man a chance of being a saint, a man of science, or an artist. But this problem cannot be attempted, much less solved, unless men desire to be these things, and if they are to desire that continuously and consciously, they must be taught what it means to be a saint, a man of science, or an artist.

What are the answers to these challenges? How will we solve these problems?

One of the solutions to our dilemma over increased enrollments lies in the noiseless revolution that has been underway for some years in the faculty structure of the Catholic schools. Today, Catholic schools in the United States employ thousands of lay teachers. The ratio in some areas of our country approximates one lay teacher to every four religious or priests. If the proportion of the total Catholic school population remains constant, it has even been predicted that by 1971 there will be more lay teachers than sisters in the parochial school system. The enrollment in the Catholic elementary schools alone is growing almost four times as fast as the number of teaching Sisters who thus far have been the mainstay of Catholic schools.

Another answer to our modern dilemma lies in an increased scholarship program. Eighty to ninety per cent of all students at the Soviet higher institutions are recipients of state scholarships. We should have the vision and the courage to embark upon an adequate scholarship aid program.

The twentieth century has witnessed many revolutions in American education. In future years we must face squarely the problems which have resulted from an education without God and without faith. Our educational scene must also be shaped by: segregation problems; universal education; the communications' revolution through the development of electronics, television, and other media; language teaching through laboratories; the identification of talent; the establishment of counseling and guidance services; and new teacher training programs. Above all we must do more to make our students understand that they have a supernatural destiny, that their spiritual capacities must be developed; that their intellects must be trained and enriched not only by the study of sciences and arts of the natural order but also by the study of revealed truth and finally they must be taught to strengthen their wills by acting against self, by prayer and the sacraments so that God and neighbor will be their first loves.

These are some of the challenges which should be faced by today's educators. There is no time or space in Almighty God, for He is an eternal, spiritual, supreme Being. And yet, in a unique age—an Age of Space—the teacher must speak of One Who is everywhere. At this point of time in history, all teachers must exemplify God's timeless qualities.

Christian Intellectuals—

Active in the Mystical Body

Thomas Aquinas [1] is one of the greatest intellectuals which our Western civilization has yet produced.

His achievements in life were many: he was a learned theologian, a profound philosopher, an able controversialist, a gifted poet, and a prodigious writer. But the chief reason why the Church honors him lies in none of these attainments. It is found in the simple fact that he was a saint.

---

[1] Given to the Harvard-Radcliffe Catholic Club on the Feast of St. Thomas Aquinas.

Education with all the concentration and endless effort that it demands is intended to develop scholars. The fundamental purpose of Catholic Club is to help souls become saints. With this two-fold equipment, intellectuality and sanctity, students should be prepared to face in the future the ultimate problems of human destiny and to do so in spiritual terms intelligible to our generation. Surely there is some means, in addition to those that have been tried, of resolving the modern, complicated problems that confront us. Those means are in the hands, heart and mind of every Christian. St. Thomas Aquinas shows us the way—prayer and study. Pray to him for guidance while I endeavor to describe your high vocation as an educated Christian.

The Christian is a member of the Body of Christ. He shares the life and the energies of that Body. He shares its function in the world and its work.

The Body to which the Christian belongs is by nature dynamic. That is, its nature is to grow in the world, to extend the teachings of Christ. The Christian intellectual is thus called to be apostolic, sharing the nature of the Body as the branches share the nature of the Vine.

The business of the Church is to convert the world. Therefore the business of the Christian is to convert the world. There is no escaping this fact; there is no softening its implications or denying its obligations.

The world for each one is the range of his personal associations and influence, the people he knows. That range must be the range of his apostolate. It is there that the Christian intellectual can and must make his contribution to solving the problems of our times. It is there that the reformation of the world, the restoration of all things in Christ, is begun. It is accomplished where we are, in all the innumerable little worlds entered or occupied by Christ through the life and action of His local members.

This is the responsibility of the Christian intellectual, that, according to his talent and range of influence, Christ depends upon him to complete the work for which Christ Himself lived and died. The intellectual, like every Christian, can hinder the work of redemption or he can continue the saving mission of his Lord. He must do one or the other. There is no neutral position. He is either with his God or against Him. To be passive is to be against Christ, for Christ depends upon Christians to continue His task. Passivity in the members of Christ's Body is a denial of their nature and a refusal of graces specifically given for the task that God created us and Christ redeemed us to do.

We get the world we earn. We can be done with war, with much evil which now besets us, though each individual and each generation must meet again the consequences of original sin: the darkened understanding, the weakened will. Still, Christ taught us to pray daily: "Thy Kingdom come, Thy will be done, on earth as it is in Heaven." The City of God is not a distant dream. The City of God can be created by each one first in himself and then among his neighbors. If enough are true citizens of the City, it appears; if not, it remains in heaven.

The difficulty is that while most of us—especially, perhaps, intellectuals—are ardent to reform our neighbors, few of us are eager to tackle ourselves, the one and only part of the world that we can assuredly conquer for Christ. Yet quite obviously there is no other sort of reform worth anything. The institutions of men and their societies express social values and actions of the men who compose or create them. The good society grows from the good in men: the evils of society grow from the evil in men. This is the first necessary premise for the understanding of the troubles of our times.

Recent revolutions, political and social, have brought startling and far-reaching changes in the history of man. From them have flowed vast consequences for his spiritual and moral life. The pattern of life which was developed slowly through the Christian era of the West is now largely dissolved.

Few men have the energy of mind and will to understand these changes. Most prefer to talk in the blindness of old mental habits. Christians, and above all scholars, must somehow be roused from these habits and impelled to rule the changing patterns rather than merely riding with them.

The situation of the Christian now has only one parallel: the first years of the Church when a few men brought the good tidings of ideas which transformed men and nations. The early Christian knew what Christians through later, more comfortable centuries largely forgot: that the Church is essentially missionary, apostolic, revolutionary. But once Christian beliefs and values prevailed, the work of priests and parish became largely to conserve these, not to spread or vitalize them. The apostolic life of the Church came to be thought of as a remote activity in missions to parti-colored pagans. But now, as in apostolic times, the pagans are of our own color and they constitute our own society; they may be members of our own families. The mission-field today begins at the church doors, at the doors of our homes, and the campuses of our Universities. In each once-Christian neighborhood there are tasks and adventures beyond the vision or the grasp of the conservatism that has lost the advancing world, but which would have been familiar to a revolutionary like Saint Paul or a religious genius like Saint Francis Xavier.

Let's face it: Christianity was once the center of gravity of our civilization. Today it is a peripheral activity. At work, in leisure, in its social, sexual, intellectual interests, the mass of the modern community is almost without traces of Christian values. Christianity is external to that community; it is remote, detached, unrealized. The Church has great institutions and organizations, but these represent partly an inheritance from the past and partly the energies of a minority within a minority. Christ's members are on the defensive in most places, on the decline in some, on the upgrade in only a few.

The problem is to renew the apostolic spirit. The Church must repenetrate the modern community from which she has been largely isolated. The community will not come to her. She must go to it, as Paul went and Xavier and Francis of Assisi. It is upon her intellectuals that she must depend for her mission in an age so enamored of ideas.

This is the necessity which has produced a growing number of priests and laymen who no longer rely on the outmoded machinery of human organization in the Church; who are no longer content with the snug security that too often shuts Christians off from real knowledge of the forces at work in the communities of which they are members but to which they seem alien. That knowledge has to be won in shops, offices, factories, forums and marketplaces.

Therefore, we have called again and again for a lay apostolate to serve in the factories, in the washrooms, theaters, newspaper offices, kitchens, camps, colleges, forums, and marketplaces of the world, to learn there and to teach there. This apostolate must be at most points the job of laymen. It must express itself much less in words than in Christian life logically and loyally lived out.

In this way can the seed be planted anew within the mass of humanity which has succeeded the ancient societies of Christendom. The Christian community must be reborn and regrown within the world community. Desocialized, the mass is straining towards some shape, some order. It must and will find organization, good or evil. Its struggle towards coherence is part of the agony of our times. It accounts for our obsession with politics, with Statism, with Communism. For Christians the task is to bring to the struggling mass the Christian spirit which, informing it, may restore it in Christian order.

We have much dead timber in our organizations and much mere formalism in our habits of mind, especially in the habit which regards our chief task as being merely to conserve. The Church is a dynamic, not a static institution. It is constantly losing ground or gaining. It cannot be frozen in set forms. There are essentials of its life but beyond these there must always be innovation, invention, enterprise, new vision. The talent of which the Gospel speaks must always be traded and never buried in safe little holes. It must be traded in the human world about us, in the places where we are and work, not merely in those where we meditate and pray. No Christian intellectual can escape the responsibility for influence on his generation. There can be no retreat from it, no ivory tower.

The Christian should never fall into the delusion of the mechanists. We may create practical machinery for specific purposes. A Federal program, a community set-up, a United Nations Organization, have many uses and to these we must give discerning, loyal support. They may curb the drug traffic, provide a police force for the world, implement some other proximate objectives, local or international.

But they cannot cure the pain in the heart of mankind, the misery, the doubts, the fears, the hatreds which grow from the negation in man of his own good, as the Christian intellectual, whatever his craft or calling, has come to see that good. Only Christ can heal, restore and renew the true good life of man. But Christ bends Himself to man. He works for men through men. Men are His instruments of salvation for men. This is what it is to be a Christian: to be a member, one with Christ, identified with His mission.

The restoration of this sense of our mission and its expression through us is the answer, and the only answer, to the world's agony and confusion. There is a solution to that agony. It is in our power. God grant us grace to play our parts well! Our salvation depends on it. So does that of America— and the world.

The Vocation of the Scientist

Some years ago speaking to a meeting of officers and men of the C.I.O. in the City of Boston I began my address with the words: "I belong here." My credentials are different when I speak on 'Science and Religion.' I speak as the representative of a Church which has always encouraged the cultivation of the arts and sciences. I am proud to be able to salute as my brothers in Christ the following bishops, priests or clerics who served God and His Church through Science:

St. Albertus Magnus (1206-1286) Dominican, Bishop, Doctor of the Church and heavenly patron of all those engaged in the natural sciences. He proved by his wonderful work that science and faith can flourish harmoniously among men.

St. Bede, Benedictine (672-735). Probably the first canonized Saint to publish research based on personal observations.

Bishop Nicholaus Steno (1638-1686). Famed as a biologist and as a geologist. The cause for his beatification has been introduced to the Holy See.

Bishop Robert Grosseteste of Lincoln (1175-1253) who with his pupil, the Franciscan Roger Bacon, is now recognized as the founder of the English school of experimental science in the 13th century

Dom Gregor Mendel (1822-1884), Augustinian abbot and father of modern genetics.

Father Angelo Secchi (1818-1878), Jesuit Astronomer of the Roman college and pioneer of modern astrophysics.

Canon Nicholas Copernicus (1473-1543), cleric and canon of Frauenburg. He was not a priest but served his bishop as cleric, lawyer, medical doctor, and diplomat who produced a plan to reform and revitalize astronomy by introducing the system which bears forever his name.

Some assert that strong religious convictions inhibit free inquiry, that only those who start from an atheistic or materialistic position are truly free from bias and that they alone can hope to attain the truth. We share our belief in God and in the supernatural order with Kepler, Galileo, Newton, Ampere, Pasteur and Marconi in addition to those already mentioned. Surey the achievements of these outstanding men of science are not in any way inferior to those of non-believers.

I have watched with interest the marked increase in recent years in the research projects and grants for study awarded to our Catholic institutions, the increasing number of scholarships in our diocesan, state and national science and merit programs, and the constant and continually increasing attention paid to graduate study and research. All this is a far cry and a great advance from the early days of Catholic education in New England. We must never forget to look back with gratitude to our immigrant ancestors who built so wisely and well, who prayed and sacrificed and worked so long and hard to establish our Catholic school system. Much has been done—much, much more, if we shall be faithful to the vision of those who preceded us, remains to be done.

Since I am not a scientist, let us consider 'Science and Religion' not from the standpoint of apologetics where we show that there is no con-

flict between true science and religious truths but
from the point of view of the apostolate. To be
specific let us speak about the *vocation* of the
scientist.

More students must be encouraged to consider
the vocation of the scientist, its importance for our
own time and its significance for eternity. Many
more must come to hear and heed the challenge to
work and teach in scientific fields. And why? Is it
because the Russians are encouraging science and
we should do likewise? No, 'me-too-ism' will not be
enough for building a life dedicated to scholarship
and research with the sacrifices which are required.
Why then? Is it for the financial rewards? No indeed, for all the present evidence indicates that
wealth will for some time to come continue to be
accumulated in the traditional manner in the mar-
kets of trade and commerce and not on the lecture
platform or the research lab. Why then? Because
the work of the scientist is really a mission which
ranks among the most noble; for scientists are called
to be the discoverers of the intentions of God in His
universe.

Sometimes people think of scientists as wizards
and magicians who, given time, can achieve what
has always seemed impossible or again they are
looked upon as 'gadgeteers,' 'tinkerers' and 'button-
pushers.' Both points of view miss the truth and
nobility of the scientist's vocation and both of these

attitudes can be dangerous and harmful for the fostering of vocations to the scientific fields. Another misapprenhension is the suspicion that somehow or other science is anti-Christian or, at best, non-Christian and that it can have no role to play in the world mission of the Church.

The Church, on the other hand, considers the mission of the scientist to be a noble one, because to share in the exploration and explanation of the wonders of God's creation is one of the highest ways of praising God: through understanding what God has made. This is what elevates the work of the scientist far above the material things with which he works: his mission is to be an *interpreter of nature* and the *guide who can teach others* to appreciate and admire God's creation while at the same time adoring the Creator with greater fervor and humility.

Let us consider this twofold aspect of the scientist's vocation: he is called to *interpret* and to *guide*.

God has spoken to man in two great books: Sacred Scripture and the book of nature. One may speak of these as supernatural and natural revelation. Since God is the Author of both and is Himself Truth there cannot be a contradiction or conflict between the two. The mission of interpreting Sacred Scripture authoritatively belongs to the Church The mission of the scientist is to interpret the book of nature. He must examine each detail, formulate a picture of its development and origin, study its relation with other details and sometimes draw consequences from this study which will be of benefit to all. In delving into the secrets of natural phenomena the scientist can provide insights which cannot be derived from any other source. And while it is certainly true that these secrets are not to be compared in nature, magnitude or importance with the sublime mysteries of supernatural revelation, still they have significance, for they allow us to discover the intentions of God in His creation and to find in the language of figures and formulae new evidence for the loving kindness and wisdom of the Almighty. Our late Holy Father, Pope Pius XII spoke of this function of the scientist as "interpreter of nature" in the following words delivered to the Pontifical Academy of Scientists:

"Your life, consecrated as it is to the study of natural phenomenon, enables you to observe every day more closely and to interpret the wonders which the Most High has inscribed on the reality of things.

"In fact, the created world is a manifestation of the wisdom and goodness of God, for all things have received their existence from Him and reflect His grandeur. Each of them is, as it were, one of His words and bears the mark of what we might call the fundamental alphabet, those natural and universal laws derived from yet higher laws and harmonies which the labor of thought strives to discover in all their fullness and their character.

"Created things are words of truth which themselves, in their being, include neither contradictions nor confusion, always cohering with one another, sometimes difficult to understand because of their depth but always, when clearly known, in conformity with the superior exigencies of nature. Nature opens up before you like a mysterious but astonishing book, requiring to be turned over page by page and read in an orderly manner with the aim in mind of progressing ceaselessly. In this manner every forward step is a continuation of the preceding ones, corrects them and climbs continually toward the light of a deeper understanding."

As a faithful interpreter, the scientist will be humble in his own discoveries because he knows the limits of his own abilities. Ere long he sees that the infinite wisdom of his Creator has been working wisely and well in His universe many billions of years before the scientist came upon the scene. As interpreter he will realize that there are problems and questions which his own science cannot answer. He will be aware that his own branch of specialized knowledge, while devoted wholly to the truth, does not itself contain all truth. He will learn as he reflects on the powers and limitations of his own science, that many of the truths which will satisfy his desire for knowledge, lie on higher planes than those of scientific research. This realization does not dampen his zeal for the exploration of nature but saves him from many pitfalls (not the least of which can be the tragic error of forgetting that it is God and not himself who is Creator, that it was God and not himself who is the Author of the book of nature).

As a reliable interpreter he knows that scientific truth becomes a decoy from the moment it is considered adequate to explain everything. It is the privilege and mission, of the interpreter, to 'look in' as it were on the act of creation as it is revealed in his own science. So, for example, in the studies of modern astronomy he looks out in space and back in time to trace the origin and development of stellar systems which are billions or sometimes only millions of years old. So too, the physicist and chemist behold the continuous changes in structure and properties of atoms and molecules which are the building blocks of the universe. And the biologist 'looks in' on the growth and development of life from the virus through the plant and animal kingdoms to man.

We have all been amazed at the swift pace which has marked man's entrance into the Age of Space since October 4, 1957, the Feast of St. Francis of Assisi, when the Russian scientists sent the first artificial satellite into orbit. Successive launchings by American and Russian teams have been most exciting and merit the attention and admiration of all. Still we cannot pass over some of the advances in both physical and life sciences which have marked as outstanding the years since 1950:

1. The discovery and application of the Salk Vaccine to counter polio.

2. The developments in the science of electronics and radio technique with such marvels as the transistor.

3. The great progress in aerodynamics and jet propulsion which make travel to almost any part of the world less than a day's journey.

4. Continuing investigations of nuclear energy in its application for peaceful purposes.

There are many things, wonderful in God's universe, and yet none of these is more wonderful than man.

At first sight man seems to be lost in the vast cosmos in which he finds himself. For he stands like some tiny mote on a small cinder which moves around an average sized star, which itself is one of some hundred billion suns in the Milky Way galaxy, while the Milky Way itself is one of some three or four trillion gallaxies which can be observed with modern astronomical equipment. Yet, when we reflect on this, we can see that the most amazing feature in all the scientific advances of the past years has not been the tremendous forces released

from atomic nuclei, nor the gigantic masses of matter which make up our sun and Milky Way, nor the
tremendous cosmic distances, nor Salk vaccine, tran-
sistors, the super jets, but rather this fact: that man,
such a tiny mote in the universe, bound within strict
limits of bodily condition and sense perception, can
reach out and make all this somehow his own, can
devise methods and instruments which increase the
power and precision of his sense measurements,
and can use his intelligence to discover the laws
which are at work in so many wondrous phenomena of nature. All these marvels of modern science
proclaim with splendid clarity the loving kindness
of our Creator who, from the slime of the earth, by
His own special creative act formed man to His own
Image. Here was a creature with a mind to ex-
plore and investigate, to enjoy and employ the
beauties and marvels of the rest of creation. Here
was an intelligent person who could read God's
book of nature and discover the intentions of God
in His universe. Here was man, God's masterpiece
in creation, the steward appointed by God to use
the other created things of this world for His praise
and reverence and service. "What is man that You
are mindful of him or the son of man that You visit
him? With glory and honor You have placed him
over all the works of Your hands."

More than this, in the mystery of the Incarnation, the Creator becomes incarnate in the uni-

verse. The Creator lay in a crib; the Author of life dies on a cross. God inserts Himself into His creation. Now the whole universe has a new meaning. Wonderfully created from nothing, it is more wonderfully sanctified by Christ's coming. He is the Creator, King of Glory, Whose coming all creation has longed for, Whose praise all creation sings: "The Heavens declare the glory of God."

By the incarnation God did not hesitate to take an earthly body for Himself. Therefore atoms, molecules, and human cells should be objects of great significance and curiosity to the Christian, for these constituents of the human body were held in hypostatic "union with the Divinity for the thirty and three years of Our Lord's life on earth and they are still united to the Person of the Divine Word in Heaven. Matter therefore is not an evil thing, it is good and it has a role to play in the drama of salvation. The duty of the Christian is to spiritualize it and bring it to the peak of perfection God wants it to have when He comes at the end of the world."

Thus man, far from being dwarfed in the universe (though in terms of matter and energy he matters very little), is God's steward charged by Him to use the other created things of this world for God's praise and glory, for his own salvation and the sanctification, peace and prosperity of his fellow man. And the scientist also has a special role: to be the interpreter of the book of nature. To do this properly he must be ready to set aside all personal prejudices and bias and to devote himself resolutely and generously in the service and quest of truth. Here is the challenge set by Pope Pius XII to the scientists of Italy:

"The assiduous realization of the maxim: *Vitam impendere vero* (*To devote one's life to Truth*), the untiring dedication to the service of science, the fight for the conquest of still more perfect knowledge as well as the systematic application to the exigencies of life—all this constitutes a *mission* from which leaders in the scientific field cannot withdraw without irreparable loss for country and people."

A high calling this: the vocation of a Catholic scientist and one which deserves our encouragement, blessing and active support.

It should be evident therefore that he who wishes to work in scientific fields and to become an 'interpreter of the book of nature' must undergo a thorough and rigorous training. There is no substitute for competence in the professional life of the scientist. The young scientist will serve his apprenticeship in magnificent halls of learning and will be convinced in double quick time that even with the best of modern facilities, there is no swift and smooth highway to success in scientific work, except the "sheer plod" which leads, uphill all the way, to the summit. The moral virtues alone can never be admission cards to the ranks of scientific excellence. Piety never dispenses with technique. No one obliges the Christian to busy himself in science, art or philosophy, for other ways of serving God are not wanting. Once, however, the choice is made of serving God through work in science then the goal itself: the investigation of the wonders of God's magnificent creation, binds one to strive for excellence. "Always to excell"–as the motto of a Jesuit college reminds us.

Those who enter scientific fields should know beforehand that they are to participate in an exciting and exacting adventure as they learn to 'discover the intentions of God' in His universe. From this it will follow that nothing but the best possible preparation for this work will be sufficient.

We have considered the vocation of the scientist as *"interpreter of nature"*; let us now pass to the role of the scientist as *"guide for others."* Here we can see in full splendor the apostolic value of scientific work. For the halls of science today can scarcely be thought of as ivory towers secluded from the pathways of men. On the contrary today's scientist is always teaching others: in the classroom and laboratory, through his publications and papers delivered at scientific meetings, in his daily contacts with friends, colleagues and neighbors. Pope Pius XII expressed it this way:

"Authorized interpreters of nature, you should also be the guides who explain to your brothers the wonders which are unfolded in the universe and which you better than others can see assembled as in a single book."

The truth is that the great majority among us cannot devote ourselves to the studious examination and contemplation of nature and must so often be content with the surface appearance of things. But those who are called to be *"interpreters of nature"* can and should also be *"teachers,"* ready and willing to reveal the beauty and power and perfection in the created world which can be enjoyed by all.

No man is an island is especially true of the scientist. More and more his expert's opinion will be sought not only for important policy decisions connected with his field of specialization but also to answer the legitimate questions put to him by men who have not had his opportunities but do have that natural desire all men have to learn.

"Teach them to behold, to understand, to love the created world so that the admiration of splendors so sublime may cause the knee to bend and raise the minds of men to adoration."

That is what Pius XII thought of the mission and vocation of the scientist. For besides using the forces of nuclear or solar energy for the service of God by bringing peace and prosperity to mankind, man can, through science, employ all creatures in the praise of God. All things praise Him Who gave them being and Who keeps them in existence. This praise becomes articulate when man, God's steward in the universe, understands the other creatures of the universe and uses his knowledge to praise Him. That troubadour of the Lord, St. Francis of Assisi, might well rejoice today and add satellites, jets and atomic engines to his 'Canticle of Praise.' For the world is charged with the grandeur of God. We have but to open our eyes to behold it, and lift up our hearts to adore Him, our Creator and Lord. Think of the happiness which you can bring to others when you can open for them some of the mysteries of nature and bring them to appreciate the magnificence of creation.

The Vatican Observatory at Castel Gandolfo, the summer residence of the Holy Father, is one of the oldest observatories in Europe and one of the best equipped. When Pope Pius XI transferred the observatory from the Vatican to the higher and clearer site in the Alban Hills he gave to the Observatory a motto which may well summarize the activity and apostolate of the scientist. The Pope had this motto carved in marble and placed with his own coat of arms over the entrance of the main dome: *Deum Creatorem Venite Adoremus*: (God the Creator, come let us adore Him.) This could well be written over the door to every laboratory (or better still inscribed in the hearts of those who work there), for it epitomizes not only for the astronomer but for all scientists the sum and scope of their works: the praise and service of their Creator through the patient and careful study of some portion of His wonderful creation.

Through microscopes and test tubes, slide rulers and computers, with hands and minds and hearts let creation praise God. The Psalmist praised Him by singing the wonders of His universe. So too did St. Francis. So also St. Ignatius in his magnificent "Contemplation for Divine Love." Let your painstaking labors, your difficult toil, your long apprenticeship in the halls of science, be spurred on by the noble purpose you have in your study of nature:–that these things of creation through you and through those you may assist as 'interpreters' or 'guides' of the book of nature may always praise, love and adore Him.

Education–A Supernatural Work

At times our Catholic educational system has been called un-American. Truth to tell, the system is rooted in the best, the original and the most American educational traditions.

Ask any historian what was the original authentic American idea of education. He will quickly refer you to the Founders of the American nation, telling you that the only education which recommended itself to them as the right kind of education for Americans was an education based on religion; and that, unhesitating in this belief, they proceeded to develop an educational system guided by it from primary school to university.

He will take you back with him to colonial days and show you a decree of the General Court of the Massachusetts Bay Colony, in 1654, where you may read that:

"forasmuch as it greatly concerns the welfare of the country that the youth thereof be educated not only in good literature, but in sound doctrine."

therefore

"in teaching, educating or instructing of youth or children in college or the schools, (no persons might engage) that have manifested themselves unsound in the faith, or scandalous in their lives, and not giving due satisfaction according to the rules of Christ."

There is no doubt that for these early colonists, education was to be based on religion. The historian will also tell you that this was a general colonial tenet, culminating in the founding of some of our greatest universities in the same spirit.

Having reminded you of many other evidences of the true idea of American education, your historian will proceed, if you wish, to conduct you step by step through the disappointing developments of the nineteenth century in American education, in which the true, the authentic and wholesome American idea of education was obscured; down to our own century when the net result of this abandonment of religion in education has been the release among us of the spirit of atheism and secularism, and the consequent creation of grave danger for our democracy.

Your historian can show you also, down through the nineteenth century and up to today, certain groups of educators who have never lost the original American idea of education, and have never abandoned it even in the face of almost insuperable difficulty. He can point to Lutherans, and Episcopalians and Presbyterians, and others, and outstanding among all these, because of the hardships they have endured, educators in the Catholic American tradition, foremost protagonists of the authentic American idea.

Let not, therefore, your work ever be called un-American. Nothing falser could be uttered. This falsehood is heard, more often by implication than by direct statement in our own day. Facing it, we who know that religion is properly the very core of American education, must not be dismayed by the opposition.

We are in line with the best educational traditions when we make religion the integrating subject to which all other subjects are related. In its relationship to the schools' curriculum it should be the strongest, the pivotal department. See to it, therefore, my dear teachers, that you keep religion in the atmosphere of the school and in the teaching of every class.

No schools are more devoted to American principles and American institutions and American traditions than Catholic schools. Equally as competent as other schools in the training of the mind they also endeavor to fashion and to form the wills of their students in the hope that they will reproduce, insofar as it is humanly possible, their Divine model, Christ our Lord.

Our relationship with the public school system has always been ideal. We have been mutually helpful. We have been partners in a great work. In every contact with every variety of school we have had the most cordial relations. People of all faiths appreciate our aims. The nation and the State value, I am sure, our contribution to the training of good citizens and the tax-payer, already overburdened, is certainly grateful for the relief we have given him.

Your model as a teacher is Christ, the Divine Teacher. The compelling charm of His divine character must be the inspiration of your work as teachers, for even in the art of teaching, He is your model and guide. What a wonderful teacher He was! Although the ideas which He expounded to the simple peasants of Galilee were sublime and superhuman, He brought them down to the intellectual level of His hearers by a wealth of simple and homely illustrations. Anyone who studies His method in the art of expression will be struck by His marvelous power of creative description. Have you ever noticed He avoids generic terms? Instead of "animals" He speaks of foxes and ravens and sparrows. Instead of "plants" He points to the mulberry trees, the fig trees and mustard seed. It was not His custom to speak of "money" but of pennies and talents.

The illustrations for His teaching were always taken from the treasury of the daily experiences of His hearers—the lilies of the field that spread before them, the sparrows that twittered among them, the vineyards that covered the slopes beside them. And His incomparable parables! He so enriched them with masterly references to things that are simple and usually unnoticed that the effortless sublimity of those stories places them amongst the greatest things of human literature. The earnest student of the Gospels cannot fail to realize that Christ is the Supreme Teacher of all time, and one who can speak to us of the most secret and divine thoughts with that natural ease and familiarity which is used by others when speaking of their personal experiences or their daily business.

We who are called upon to continue Christ's work of imparting the knowledge of divine things to children must imitate the example of the Divine Teacher by trying to make our instructions living and real, simple and sincere, rich with the truth and vibrant with human interest.

Let us never forget, however, that our first duty is to mould Christ-like characters. Having made Christ live in our own lives we must spend ourselves to make Him live in our pupils. In your classroom work, and in preparation for it, the all-engrossing new features and trends in the field of education may seem to demand the first place and the most attention. But the most helpful, the most inspiring, the most thrilling thing, the one necessary thing is the contagious Christ-like character of the teacher. Your professional preparation, your degrees, your pedagogical technique, whatever may be needed to comply with the highest standards, all these are exacted chiefly that you may be qualified to teach secular subjects and prepare your pupils for place and competency in this passing life. They must not be neglected.

But, as Catholic teachers, your fundamental duty is to form Christ in the minds and hearts and souls of the little ones. You must enlighten them and strengthen them to say with the Apostle: "It is not now I who live, but Christ liveth in me." You must prepare them to let their light so shine before men that they may see their radiant goodness and be led by their example to glorify the Heavenly Father.

You can do this only if you can say that Christ lives in you. You can do this only if your little men and women can see your good works, the devotion and patience of the teaching Christ, the kindness and sweet strength of the teaching Christ, the holiness, the goodness, the love of the teaching Christ in your faces and poise, see these in your every work and gesture. Through your likeness to Christ which they will contemplate, they will be transformed into like resemblance. This likeness, however, you must first achieve yourselves by meditation on the Christ life, by living always in His presence, by looking into His face. St. Paul has given us assurance that by "beholding the glory of the Lord with open face we are transformed into the same image, as by the spirit of the Lord." Try, therefore, dearly beloved teachers, try more and more to put on Christ," to be perfect, to be holy—holy—holy.

In our busy age when educational ideals are sadly secularized and competition in secular learning is most acute, the worldly-wise would counsel you to shorten your prayers, your meditations, your spiritual reading, your intimate communions with God in order that you may double your toil. But I appeal to you to resist that temptation. The work of education to which you have consecrated your lives is a supernatural work, and its first aim is to produce supernatural men and women. Therefore, renew during the most solemn moments of the Mass, your determination to take no lower model for your educational guidance than the Divine Teacher.

Realization of the Catholic Ideal

Reverend William F. Cunningham, C.S.C., professor of Education at the University of Notre Dame, reiterated and clarified the primary purpose of Catholic education when he wrote: "The specific, essential function of the Catholic College is the development of its students as contributing citizens in a free society, and as apostolic members of the Church." Having laid down this precept Father Cunningham specifies "what college is not." "A college," he says, "is not a clinic or a hospital, though

154

it will safeguard the health of its students and promote vigorous living on the campus as the best guarantee of health in later life."

"It is not an orphan asylum or a home, but it will manifest paternal solicitude for the well-being of its students and exercise a fatherly care in all spheres of life."

"A college is not a farm or factory, nor a store or office, but it will give a fundamentally broad training that will prepare its students to become efficient producers of goods or services."

"A college is not a park or a country club, but it will have a well-planned program of social activities and physical education, (including both intramural and intercollegiate athletics), giving its students in their leisure hours relief from their work, which is study."

"A college is not a monastery or a church, but it will have a vital religious program which, in addition to the development of intellectual virtues through the curriculum, will develop the moral virtues through private devotions and public worship with active participation in the liturgy of the Church."

This is a terse way of expressing the first part of the twofold purpose of a Catholic college. It all adds up to the fact that something very Catholic has been brewing in Catholic education groups in our country for more than a decade now. Over and over again, we hear dogmatically poured forth the truth: Theology, with philosophy as a handmaid, must be the unifying principle of our curriculum. Does it stop there? Or are we really doing something about it?

It were well here to refer to the classical encyclical on education of Pope Pius XI, namely, *The Christian Education of Youth.* He says: "Indeed there has never been so much discussion about education as nowadays; never have exponents of new pedagogical theories been so numerous, or so many means devised, proposed, and debated, not merely to facilitate education, but to create a new system infallibly efficacious, and capable of preparing the present generations for that earthly happiness they so ardently desire.

"It is as important to make no mistake in education, as to make no mistake in the pursuit of the last end, with which the whole work of education is intimately and necessarily connected. In fact, since education consists essentially in preparing man for what he must be and for what he must do here below in order to attain the sublime end for which he was created, it is clear that there can be no true education which is not wholly directed to man's last end, and that . . . there can be no ideally perfect education which is not Christian education."

Surely this is approval of our statement that theology should be the ultimate unifying and integrating factor of Catholic education. That it is the mind of the Church that the principles of theology should guide and motivate all the courses of our curriculum is no new dictum. Hear this striking confirmation as defined by the Vatican Council:

"Not only is it impossible for faith and reason to be at variance with each other; they are on the contrary of mutual help. For while right reason establishes the foundations of Faith . . . Faith on the other hand frees and preserves reason from error, and enriches it with varied knowledge. The Church, therefore, far from hindering the pursuit of the arts and sciences, fosters them in many ways . . . . Nor does she prevent the sciences, each in its sphere, from making use of methods and principles of their own . . . . She takes every precaution to prevent them from falling into error by opposition to divine doctrine . . . and thus invading and disturbing the domain of Faith."

Substitute for "science" in the preceding passage any other course in our curriculum and we have the attitude of the Church on all branches of liberal education. "In fact," Pope Pius XI says, "it must never be forgotten that the subject of Christian education is man whole and entire . . . . Christian education takes in the whole aggregate of human life, physical and spiritual, intellectual and moral, individual, domestic and social, . . . in order to elevate, regulate, and perfect it. . . . Hence the true Christian, the produce of Christian education, is the supernatural man who thinks, judges, and acts consistently in accordance with right reason, illumined by the supernatural light of the example and teaching of Christ; in other words, to use the current term, he is the true and finished man of character."

It is theology, then, together with philosophy, that forms the structure of the synthesis which should be the pattern of a genuine Catholic education. I should like to submit here a typical modern program in theology and philosophy based on the Thomistic synthesis. It runs like this: *First Year*: God and His World, . . . a course covering the first part of Saint Thomas' *Summa*,—God in His nature and in the Trinity of Persons, God the Creator. It covers in philosophy the subject matter of theodicy and rational psychology. *Second Year*: the moral life of man, which embraces the course of ethics in philosophy and far beyond. *Third Year*: devoted to the life of virtue, is in reality a course in special ethics. Morality is considered not as a series of don'ts but as a positive program leading to the acquisition and intensification of the virtues necessary for salvation. *Fourth Year*: considers Christ the God-Man, Who is our way to God. In natural sequence follows a consideration of Christ's Sacraments, and the other means of salvation. In addition to his integrated study of philosophy and theology the student takes logic, courses in general and experimental psychology, metaphysics or cosmology.

How does this integration work into the other departments of the college? Here, I must admit again that it is necessary for the philosopher and the theologian to work side by side with the expert in methods, with the technician, with the professors of content courses. Thus shall we bring into our work of education the fullness of our Catholic educational ideal. Religion must, indeed, be the core if the ideals of Catholic education are to be fully realized. This may be accomplished if school faculties can be led to see the importance of meeting regularly, and with religion as the center of their thinking, agree through cooperative planning on the part each department may play in directing the total program toward worthy Christian living. Let us give thought to the observation made some years ago by Robert Hutchins when he put his finger on the spot and said that the chief thing wrong with Catholic education was that it was not Catholic enough! In other words, he was trying to tell us that the only education which is real education is that which makes use of the perfect unifying and integrating reality which is found only in Catholic theology.

Let us consider the second point of our proposed twofold purpose of Catholic higher education; namely, to perfect the soul and its life of grace;

to perfect nature and all that pertains to it, since the one presupposes the other. In many cases the groundwork for this point has been laid in Catholic elementary and secondary schools. Consideration of this second item awakens in us a deep concern that education should strive to perfect human beings in all the relevant circumstances of their earthly lives. Perfecting the soul and its life of grace implies a wide scope of education. It is a stimulating challenge to Catholic education. To approach it, to accomplish all that it requires, teachers of religion, primarily—and all professors in their own departments—need a thorough understanding of youth and an interest in all that concerns them. All our teachers need a full understanding of the great problems of our complex society; they need to teach Christian attitudes and to relate Christian social principles to the subjects and techniques which they are teaching.

If this seems to exaggerate the role of the teacher of religion, I can only say that this is an era in which we need to be much more realistic in our consideration of religion programs. We no longer live in the Ages of Faith when most people learned and lived religion in the home and in society. We live at a time when homes and society in general have lost spiritual force, and when, therefore, schools must assume a wider responsibility in order that Christian homes and civic life may be restored to full strength. All of this is a means of carrying out the second point of the twofold purpose of a Catholic College, viz., to perfect the soul and its life of grace; to perfect nature and all that pertains to it.

When we review the havoc wrought by the education sponsored by every totalitarian form of government, we are convinced that millions of the youth under such domination receive an education devoid of morality. How much more concerned should we not be then to see that our students are instructed in the truths of God, in the principles of morality—truths and principles that are not only Catholic but American?

If in our colleges, in all departments, our professors will inculcate principles of morality and those habits of restraint which will make our students virtuous men and women, those same principles will help to make them useful, law-abiding citizens, and ornaments of our democracy. This will be the result of our striving to fulfill the twofold purpose of a Catholic college.

Moral training of youth must not be planned for him alone. If as a social being he is to be trained for citizenship, his will must be trained to adhere to the principles which reason tells him are those of right living. He must be trained to do *not what everyone does, but what he knows to be right.* He must be trained to develop a deep sense of responsibility, a respect for authority, an abiding consider-

ateness for the rights of others. Indeed, the essence
of democracy is respect for the individual. This
moral training of youth—which of all sciences is the
most sublime—requires not so much the *de luxe*
methods of our modern educational regime, as it
does teachers who, while thoroughly prepared academically, are more specifically teachers grounded
in grace, grounded in the apostolic desire to cooperate with God in the salvation of souls. Their
abiding concern should be to deepen and sharpen
their own spiritual aims, to broaden their spiritual
sympathy. Theirs should be a singleheartedness in
their devotedness to their work; theirs a love of
souls; theirs an ever-increasing realization of their
responsibility in God's sight. The youth they teach
today will be the men and women of tomorrow. Everything in time and in eternity depends upon the
training received at their hands. Precept alone will
make but a fleeting impression, if students do not
sense that their professors live up to the ideals they
advocate. Such conviction will not only deepen and
strengthen their reverence for their teachers but it
will be for them a spur to progress. It is a sacred
privilege to teach students the Christian concept of
life. To do this successfully, we must make Christ
a vital part of our lives. By prayer and meditation,
we must strive daily to become more and more like
Christ in order that we may make Him live and
grow in the lives of those for whom we are respon-

sible. Personal holiness should come first in the lives of all those who are responsible for our Catholic students.

We shall not fail in forming men and women of character in our schools if we build our religious education around Christ as a center. If He is our ideal of perfect character; if we look to Him to find our supreme source of inspiration; if we mould character and life—our own and our students'—after His character and life, we shall attain the two-fold purpose of a Catholic college. The self-control, the high ideals, the sublime standards of conduct that the imitation of Christ as an ideal proposes, cannot but ennoble, cannot but inspire with a desire for sanctity the students we train. The important point is to establish an ideal in the student's intellect, Christ; and then, through the intellect, to reach the will of the student. Christ must be made a living Personality, One Whom the student is eager to know better, to love, to depend upon, with Whom he may share his joys, his sorrows, his hopes, his fears, his weaknesses, his triumphs. He should be impressed with the doctrine of the life of God in his soul when he is in sanctifying grace. Prayer should be made attractive, a necessity. We cannot stress too much for the student the need of prayer, the love of prayer. Then in maturer years, if sin should claim him, he will remember that the gate of the way back to God and happiness is always open to him, if he will but enter in through prayer. The personal love of Christ which he learned to value when under our guidance in college will be for him a saving memory. Then he will think again of Christ as his Friend. If he is weak, he will look to Christ for strength. If he is stained with sin, he will turn to the infinite sanctity of Christ, his Friend, for cleansing. Then the fire of Christ's love will inflame his coldness; the mercy of Christ's Heart will dispel his misery; the memory of the patience of Christ, which he learned from us, will give him courage to begin again.

I am convinced that if we make Christ the center of our teaching; if we depict Him as the Dynamic Leader, Friend, and Redeemer, which He is; if we make Him essential to the complete happiness of our students; then, when the storms of life rage around them, they will call to Him over the waters, and He will come to them, and they will know the peace of Christ. If they catch from us the spirit of Christ, they will become lay apostles. Then we shall find them in their homes, in offices, in professions, in the government, making moral principles known and respected. We *may* turn out brilliant graduates. We *may* produce successful men of business. We *may* send forth cultured exponents of our college training. But we *must* prepare our students by a life of virtue, by a life of grace to be true followers of Christ, potential citizens of Heaven. Then, indeed, we shall have met the challenge of Catholic education.

THE DAUGHTERS OF ST. PAUL

In Massachusetts
50 St. Paul's Ave.
Jamaica Plain
BOSTON 30, MASS.
172 Tremont St.
BOSTON 11, MASS.
381 Dorchester St.
SO. BOSTON 27, MASS.
325 Main St.
FITCHBURG, MASS.

In New York
78 Fort Place
STATEN ISLAND 1, N.Y.
39 Erie St.
BUFFALO 2, N.Y.

In Connecticut
202 Fairfield Ave.
BRIDGEPORT, CONN.

In Ohio
141 West Rayen Ave.
YOUNGSTOWN 3, OHIO

In Texas
114 East Main Plaza
SAN ANTONIO 5, TEXAS

In California
827 Fifth Ave.
SAN DIEGO 1, CALIF.

In Louisiana
86 Bolton Ave.
ALEXANDRIA, LA.

In Florida
2700 Biscayne Blvd.
MIAMI 37, FLORIDA

In Canada
33 W. Notre Dame
MONTREAL, CANADA
1063 St. Clair Ave. West
TORONTO, CANADA

In England
29 Beauchamp Place
LONDON, S.W. 3, ENG.

In India
Water Field Road—Extension
PLOT N. 143—BANDRA

In Philippine Islands
No. 326 Lipa City
PHILIPPINE ISLANDS

In Australia
58 Abbotsford Road
HOMEBUSH N.S.W., AUSTRALIA